Far From The Meadows of Ukraine

By

Joanne Overbury

Text copyright © 2024 by Joanne Overbury

All rights reserved.

No part of this book may be reproduced, or stored in a retrieval system, or transmitted in any form or by any means, electronic, mechanical, photocopying, recording, or otherwise, without the express written permission of the publisher.

Cover photo, Stockport viaduct.
Image used curtesy of Stockport Heritage Library.

Dedicated in the memory of Maria & Myroslaw, whose hard-work and commitment continues to live on in the Ukrainian community of Stockport.

Contents

1. Melodies So Pure & True......................................4
2. Falling In Love...16
3. Setting Up A Life Together................................50
4. Buying A First Home..85
5. Missing The Motherland...................................101
6. Holodomor - Death By Hunger.........................111
7. Easter..124
8. Graz -Austria..160
9. Fixing Roots...201
10. 1966..214
11. Passport Refusal...225
12. Ukraine's Independence - Safe To Return........228

About the Author...238

1
Melodies So Pure & True

Let The Bells Ring
13th November 1948

Heavy rain splattered repeatedly on the tiny windowpane. Condensation misted the narrow view onto the empty, cobbled street below. The blustering gale caused an uneasy rattle from the old wooden frame

The small bedroom filled with a beautiful, heart-warming chorus as Maria hummed a cheerful tune, drowning out, somewhat, the dreary weather outside.

Folk melodies and traditional music had always been an enormous comfort, especially over recent uncertain years. It gave the young woman a magical closeness and a memorable grasp of a safe home that once was and a family now lost. So far away from her current life, but so near and powerfully touching to her loving heart and her constant thoughts.

Apart from comforting her and granting a much-needed respite, these familiar, sweet-sounding songs had offered her the occasional moment of delight and laughter on the plentiful, grey, unpredictable days.

Upon a small, soft padded, pink stool she perched, dreamily gazing with a gentle purity into the mirror as she brushed the soft curls of her hair. Her cool, ice blue eyes shone back in return, she hardly recognised the mysterious young lady in the reflection.

The last few months had brought her such a whirlwind of unexpected, but refreshing happiness, Maria had barely had time to catch her breath.

Receiving that first letter in return post had given her such a warm contentment.

She had felt an instant connection to the sweet words he had so thoughtfully written. She immediately felt the empty, loneliness she had endured in recent years begin to ease.

Myroslaw understood.

His handwriting convinced her so, such exquisite script. It had been a long while since she had seen text in a language she could understand. Her language. A language that they shared.

This young man was obviously well educated, using sophisticated words, with an air of confidence and great meaning. It was a brief letter, short but sweet she thought; however, his few written words had spoken so much more.

It had been at the suggestion of her employers that the newly settled 'Displaced Persons' should write to the men on labour camps. These men had also recently arrived in Britain. Just like the displaced persons, they too had been obliged to flee to safety, to avoid the effects of armed conflict in their homeland, Ukraine. Both groups found themselves in similar situations, fearing they had lost their homes and family to the war.

The men were members of the 1st Ukrainian Division. After surrendering to the Allied Forces at the end of the war, they had been held captive as Prisoners of war at a coastal camp in Rimini, Italy. Here, screening to confirm their motives and whereabouts during the conflict had taken place, by both Soviet and British missions, set up by the war office. After spending two long years restricted on the camp, some 7100 men had been transferred and accommodated in prisoner of war camps around the United Kingdom, mainly being rehomed on unoccupied military land in agricultural areas.

Having become unaccustomed to a life outside of these camps, these Prisoners of War needed a great deal of support. They would certainly benefit from some guidance and a welcoming hand to help them understand the different culture and way of life in this new country.

The thought of becoming pen-pals had been an exhilarating escape from the long, tedious, days Maria was enduring at Pear Mill. Although she worked beside several pleasant women, she had only mastered a few words of the English language. So, once she had greeted her fellow workers with an 'Hello' or shown her gratitude with a 'Thank you,' the conversation soon ended.

Being the chatty, bubbly person Maria was, just wasn't possible in those surroundings so she merely kept her head down and worked mostly in silence, although the magnificent, repetitive echoes caused by the clattering of the cotton machines broke this considerably.

After a few adventurous months of exchanging these exciting but very meaningful letters, Myroslaw suggested the two of them should meet up. Maria couldn't have been more thrilled, her head swirled with excitement.

The day finally arrived and with it came a beautiful blue sky, the sun shone like glistening gold, matching her uplifted feelings for what lay ahead. An intrigued Maria, strolled cheerfully to the bus station in the town centre to meet Myroslaw. She couldn't help but smile widely to herself. At last, she was about to see the face behind those wonderful words that had filled her life so gratefully lately. She felt as though she already knew so much about Myroslaw. The quickened heartbeat in her chest, she told herself, was excitedly beating, rather than a nervous pounding.

* * *

Myroslaw had risen early from his restless sleep, wanting plenty of time to get washed and shaved in peace before the morning rush came to use the facilities. Pulling his suit jacket onto his slim body, his rough hands smoothed down the collars of his shirt. Even though he had been given good hearty meals lately on the camps, he seemed unable to rectify the months of near starvation he had endured on the concentration camp, unable to rebuild his body to what it once was.

Ready! he thought to himself as he headed off along the lane.

Thankfully, there was a bus stop just a short walk from The Heath Camp. With a daily bus heading into Lincoln. The route for the exchange bus to Maria's town had been kindly mapped out and written down by his camp officer, so Myroslaw was able to make the long and restless journey from Wellingore.

It was his day of rest, so it was a pleasant avoidance from filling his time needlessly with chatter amongst his fellow prisoner of war campmates.

Sundays were tediously long days on the camp, the men's employers—the local farmers, ran the farmland themselves on this day it seemed.

The air was quiet and peaceful without the rumble of the ploughs. However, Myroslaw preferred to be kept busy working in the fields, than having time to himself. They were allowed outside of the camp but with nowhere to go and no-one to see, anything more than a short walk out seemed pointless.

Sundays were always the same, too much spare time, too much thinking time amongst the campmates. No matter how upbeat they attempted to be, the talk always returned intensely to the dark, horrific past events that Myroslaw, amongst others, tried so hard to forget. Occasionally there would be news or gossip they had somehow managed to gather about their homeland or the whereabouts of the families they had lost or left behind.

With virtually no interaction or socialising between the local village community and camp inhabitants—partly due to the inability to communicate in English—the days with no work were long and tiresome. Although thankfully, in more recent week's male choirs and dance troops had formed. Sports activities had begun to take shape, with groups willingly forming together on the camp to have some fun times, making for a less anxious and depressed feel to this questionable future.

This was to be a special day, a time that had thankfully become trapped in his thinking in recent weeks.

Would Maria like him as much in person?

Would they have plenty to talk about?

Although they didn't have photographs of each other, they had described in their last letter exchange what they looked like.

Would he recognise her by her description?

His thoughts were abruptly interrupted a few hours into his bus journey.

"Next stop Stockport," the driver sharply announced.

This town, even on a glorious, hot, summer day, seemed a world away from the sweet smelling, green grass and abundance of fresh air he had left behind that morning.

The striking, bright yellow roses he'd so carefully nursed along the journey, seemed so out of place as they gleamed vibrantly in the dull, grey, smoky surroundings.

Huge brick industrial buildings and tall chimneys enveloped the streets. Endless clouds of smoke bellowed out into the ocean of blue sky above, bringing a shudder to Myroslaw as he fought back the memories.

Those days are finished, there's better days to be had, he thought to himself and tried to focus on the beautiful day that lay ahead.

Looking out of the window as the bus pulled into the station, he could see a beautiful young lady waiting beside the bus bay, a huge smile lighting up her face. His stomach rolled in excitement, his pulse fluttered with nerves. Each with the hope that this could be Maria. She had such kind and gentle features, her russet hair neatly clipped back away from her face, with smooth waves reaching past her shoulders, stunning eyes, like blue topaz shining in the sunshine. She was just as he had imagined.

All of this felt, to Myroslaw, simply too good to be true.

Treading down the small stairwell, he stepped off the bus, smoothed down his dark hair and took in a deep breath before he moved forward, clutching a small brown suitcase in one hand, containing the only change of shirt he possessed and a change of socks and underwear. In the other hand he gently held the sweetest smelling flowers, a perfect gift for this wonderful young woman, the woman who had given him the reason to live life to the full once again, given him hope for a life of peace, joy and happiness.

***

Maria's timid smile widened once again, as this tall and very handsome young man approached.

"Maria?" he questioned, nervously.

"Tak, yes, I am Maria," she beamed, pleased to have remembered the English phrase she had been practising.

Myroslaw leant forward into Maria's space, presented her with a cheeky but friendly kiss on the cheek and handed her the flowers, the most beautiful she'd seen in a long time. Soaking up the sweet fragrance as she held them close.

The warm, pleasant morning was spent relaxing blissfully at the nearby Alexandra Park. Passing a triangular border of giant pink hydrangeas, they found a quiet spot on the freshly cut grass and Myroslaw placed his brown suit jacket for Maria to sit on beside him.

Neither of them spoke of the horrors they had been involved in or witnessed, unsure if there would ever be a time when such emotions and terrors could be disclosed and expressed openly. Instead, they spoke of the new lives they had been granted, both privately sharing a feeling of a sheltered protection, brought upon by spending this precious time together.

An idyllic, carefree day was spent untroubled and thankful. Both secretly feeling hopeful of the promise that better times may be ahead. Although, neither had dared to dream or hope; just survive the moment, as had been the way of life for some time.

Maria had thoughtfully packed a small lunch, wrapped inside a clean blue and white gingham tea towel at the suggestion of her landlady, Elsie. She had placed it carefully inside the small handbag she had borrowed for the day from her good friend Rosa.

She prompted, after all the endless talking they'd shared, that they should maybe eat a little and Myroslaw headed towards the nearby drinks kiosk to buy them refreshments. Maria gently laid out the tea towel, exposing the aroma of the freshly baked bread rolls inside and placed beside them the thinly sliced meat and ripe tomatoes that she had brought.

She had wanted to provide a huge feast; a wonderful picnic for them to share, but with her lack of money and a shortage of products in the local shops, she had found it to be quite an impossible task.

Conversation and a great deal of laughter continued during their lunchtime and throughout the afternoon, with a giddiness of new romance and hand holding. Although to be fair, the conversation was quite one sided. Maria felt immensely relaxed in Myroslaw's company. With such a freeness in this familiar language, it was a breath of fresh air for her.

Myroslaw, a quiet man of few words, but a fantastic and thoughtful listener, was more than happy for Maria to take the lead in their conversations and found he could happily listen to her chatting all day long. He thoroughly enjoyed her company.

Hours passed and the park began to empty of its visitors.

Daylight started to fade as they slowly wandered hand in hand along Worrall Street to Maria's lodgings, neither of them wanting this perfect moment to come to an end.

Myroslaw turned to face Maria and daringly pulled her curvy waist gently towards him.

She had expected a 'Goodnight' farewell instead he questioned, "Maria, will you marry me?"

With a delighted excitement, Maria beamed a smile in reply. Of course, there was no doubt in her mind, she wanted more than anything to have the love and protection this wonderful, kind man offered, to cushion and surround her throughout her life. But she wasn't usually the daydreamer type. Life had taught her some tough lessons and made her stronger by consequence.

After all, they had literally just met in person.

Even though they had been exchanging correspondence for the last four months, sharing details of the lives they now lived, writing about the new places they visited and friends they had made, they'd also discussed how important family was to them both. How amazing it was to have someone they could share their thoughts and dreams with, even in letter form. They both looked forward to the next letter arriving. It certainly eased the loneliness. A relationship formed on paper that made them feel so close to one another.

She knew her answer but for now, it was hers to know. *One day*, she thought to herself, *yes, one day*.

A smile would have to be enough of an answer for now.

"Dobraneech," she whispered, as they hugged each other a goodnight blessing.

"Dobraneech, Maria," Myroslaw returned.

Bidding each other goodnight, they promised to meet again in a few weeks time.

Unbeknown to them both, today had been just the beginning…

Myroslaw watched as Maria closed the heavy, creaking door behind her, happy in the knowledge that she was safely returned to her lodgings. He began the short stroll to the Blue Bell Hotel. A large, imposing building in the back streets of Edgeley, where he was staying for the night, before his early morning bus trip back to the camp… back to his new reality.

Maria (right) & Rosa (left) arriving in Stockport

Myroslaw (left) & Ivan (right)
at
The Heath Camp, Wellingore

2
Falling In Love

Over the following few months, the young couple took it in turns visiting each other, meeting up on several occasions in their own towns, grabbing every opportunity to spend time together on their work free days.

Religion had always been a huge, important part of Ukrainian lives and both Maria and Myroslaw found comfort in their beliefs during their toughest of times. Although the vast fields of The Heath Camp didn't have its own church building, a section of one of the large wooden huts had been divided up by the men and cleverly adapted to create a place to hold religious and community events. Several men spent long hours carving and constructing rows of sturdy wooden pews for the seating. The camp officers had willingly supported this project, kindly providing the congregation with all the relevant reading materials and hymn books.

Early one September morning, Myroslaw waited eagerly for Maria to arrive by bus for a visit. The crisp leaves crunched on the ground as he shuffled his feet to keep warm.

He sheltered beside the hedgerow, wrapping his brown woollen jacket tightly around his slight chest, as the cool breeze swirled over the fields. The sun hadn't yet made an appearance on what promised to be a pleasant autumnal day.

Typically, he was ahead of time, he had headed towards the bus stop as soon as he had finished eating his warm porridge breakfast. Wanting to make sure he was there in plenty of time and prior to Maria's arrival.

Shortly before nine o'clock the bus whirled down the narrow country lane, pulling up briefly at the Wellingore stop.

As Maria descended the steps of the bus, Myroslaw rushed over to wrap his arms around her, the warm embrace soothing his wind-swept body slightly. His heart missed a beat in the delight of holding his lady in his arms once again.

This was how love felt.

Several displaced wives, coming from overseas and newly arrived in Britain had recently re-connected and joined their husbands on the camp. Maria was looking forward to meeting them, thrilled to have these fellow Ukrainian girls to speak with.

They were all soon chatting away, like the best of friends. Listening intently as the girls took it in turns to share their story, Maria soon discovered many of them had similar tales to her own. Iryna, a pretty girl of a similar age to Maria finished off on a happy note.

"finding my husband alive and safe in Britain had felt as special as the day we were married," she told the group.

After sharing in her happiness, the group suddenly went silent. Some looked down at the floor with sadness. They knew of the last story to be told. There was only Lesia who hadn't yet spoken. Her tired face grey and sunken, she looked to be far older than the others, although the trauma may have aged her.

The silence was broken as the last story began. Maria was brought to tears, as were the rest of them. Listening to Lesia relive the events she had survived, not knowing if she had wanted to survive, unsure if she could carry on a life with the grief and burden she carried, eating away at her every day.

Her husband, Roman had been away fighting for their country. She was at home taking care of her sick mother and young son Petro. The Germans had come marching through the village waving their rifles around and causing panic. They had been brutely ordered onto the wagons, with no idea where they were being taken. She had felt thankful that they had all been taken together. The three of them huddled together, terrified. Her mother was weak with a fever and thankfully slept for most of the journey, only waking as they were loaded onto a cattle train for their onward journey. Lesia was relieved once they arrived at their destination, thinking she could get her mother some medical help and a warm bed.

"Nee, nee," she spluttered angrily. She had been so very wrong. She began to sob heavy tears as she continued her nightmare.

As they began to disembark from the train, she'd heard mutterings around her 'Auschwitz' they were whispering over their nerves.

Jumping down from the train, she turned to help her mother and Petro down from the height. The soldiers on the platform behind her were bellowing their orders, strutting around in charge. The three of them tried to stay with the others they had travelled with, but the noise and panic had taken over. People were being pushed this way and that way. They struggled to stay together. The soldiers with their guard dogs barking viciously by their sides pushed and separated everyone.

"My Boy, Petro, he was clinging to my leg. I told him to stay holding onto me, but the soldier." She paused briefly, clearing the sorrow from her throat. "He ripped my son away from me," she continued, "and sent him to join another queue with the other children, my mother was sent another way and they both quickly disappeared from my sight." She took a breath and wiped her eyes, as she obviously had done a thousand times before. "I soon learned, that if you cried or screamed, you would pay for it I never saw them again." She broke down, huge sobs uncontrollably shaking her frail body.

She had somehow survived two traumatic years on the concentration camp. The unknown whereabouts of her young son and elderly mother were a larger torture than the beatings she had received. She was thankful to have now found her husband, grateful to be able to share with him the burdening grief she felt.

The silence resumed, within the group, only sniffles could be heard between them as the women tried to gather their thoughts. Maria reached over to Lesia, placing her caring arms around her shoulders, embracing her close to her chest. She couldn't imagine how a mother would feel losing her child. It was unbearable to think of such an event.

Later that afternoon, a service was held at the new church room to welcome them all into their new community.

This was a truly wonderful experience for Maria. She had been a regular visitor to the Catholic church close to her lodgings since her arrival to Stockport but had been unable to follow any of the services, as they were conducted in the English language. She had simply attended to feel safe and at ease in God's home. Knowing he would be listening to her prayers; she would light a candle for her family's safety and survival.

At the end of the camp service and feeling at peace, the couple decided to approach the Ukrainian Priest. He too was an inmate on the camp, Myroslaw had known him since their time at the camp in Rimini, Italy, before they had boarded for Britain. If anyone would be willing and able to help them marry, it was him.

* * *

Looking away from the mirror, Maria began gently pushing a hairbrush through her wavy hair. Imagining how her wedding morning would have been spent back home in Ukraine, surrounded by her family women. Her bridesmaids would gently comb out her plaited hair, singing as they re-braided it into a wreath on her head.

The groom and his entourage would be arriving at her parent's home, to pay a ransom for his bride. He would be carrying two loaves of bread; a gift for her family.

Closing her eyes, Maria pictured Myroslaw standing at the 'Brama', the gates of her home back in the village. A decorated table set in place, with flowers upon a special 'rushnyk' embroidered cloth outside the main entrance. On the other side of the table, the bridesmaids would gather, waiting in anticipation for the groom to state what he had come for.

"To receive my bride," he would proudly state.

He would glorify and compliment the bride, to establish her sense of worth, offering up the price of ransom in candles, money or livestock. A bride is very precious to her family, a groom can't win her easily. Marias parents would bring her outside, dressed in a beautifully embroidered wedding gown. Before the wedding party can leave for the church, a price would be agreed.

The parents would hold two icons of Jesus and the virgin Mary, before the couple, draped with a rushnyk for the blessing. Blessing them with a long, happy, and prosperous life together.

Maria suddenly heard a loud, urgent banging on the front door. Followed instantly by quick tapping footsteps along the hallway below, snatching her away from her daydream.

Elsie had been in the front parlour, searching through the rain speckled window, waiting for the visitor and had readily rushed to open the door. "Come in doll, quickly. Oh Rosa darling, you're soaked through, get yourself inside and dried off. You'll catch your death young lady." She hurried closing the door behind them to the rain.

Although she was unable to understand any of the words that had just been spoken to her, Rosa gratefully stepped inside. The warmth of the hallway rushed over her, blushing her cheeks.

Rosa and Maria had become the closest of friends. They had first met and shared a bunk on the giant ship that they anxiously travelled on the long, overnight, journey from the Hook of Holland to Harwich and into this distant country called England.

Although very little sleep had been undertaken. They both enjoyed their time spent up on the deck, watching the huge dark waves splash repeatedly in the moonlight, slowly carrying them forward to the unknown. To a place where safety, a new home and employment were being promised.

Enjoyment was soon mixed with nerves as each powerful wave pushed them further and further away from the place they lovingly called home. Further away from finding their lost families.

They had often shared how thankful they each were of their friendship. Out of all the hundreds of other displaced persons undertaking the journey, they had found each other. They believed it was God's blessing placing them together and each would be eternally grateful.

Even though, as they soon discovered, they had different homelands, their languages were slightly similar. Apart from the odd barrier, they managed to communicate quite well and had relished the emotional support each had given to the other in adjusting to this new life.

Rosa was a quiet and shy girl, but the backing and support that Maria's sunny outlook and energetic confidence gave her was very much appreciated.

Slightly older than Maria, at twenty-three years of age, Rosa was the youngest sibling within a family of nine children. She hadn't often had the opportunity to use her voice and found it easier to blend into the large family rather than try to be heard or seen.

Life now, although over thirteen hundred miles from her hometown of Lublin, Poland, and with her newfound best friend Maria by her side to brighten her day, had begun to feel like home.

Shuffling hastily out of her rain-soaked shoes, she removed the dripping coat and passed it over to an awaiting Elsie.

"Go, go girl, Maria is waiting for you, go girl, help her become the most beautiful bride, go!!" Elsie laughed merrily as she took the drenched, woollen, coat from Rosa, ushering her upstairs to Maria's bedroom.

Elsie had only known Maria for eleven months; since the day that Mrs Chamberlain from the Ministry of labour office had tottered along the pathway, in her heels and tapped keenly and efficiently on the door. She had been really unsure what to expect when agreeing to take in a lodger, not just your usual lodger, but a refugee from a country she knew nothing about, 'Ukraine'.

How would it work?
Would they speak any English language?
Would they be courteous, kind, polite.?
How old would they be?

So many unanswered questions.

She needn't have wasted any time worrying or searching for the answers, having Maria in the house had been such an unforgettable joy to both her and her husband Sid. Like the young and joyful daughter they had always dreamt about having, but sadly never been blessed with.

Maria had proven to be a real hard worker and was always keen to help with any housework chores, any cooking or baking that Elsie needed a hand with. She would breeze into the house after a long, dusty workday in the Mill and within minutes the muted silence of the day would come alive, the house would be filled with the most beautiful singing or humming from her bedroom above.

Sid would regularly be out at his local pub, *The Armoury*. He must have been the only customer that wasn't over keen on alcohol. He wasn't there to waste his money on drink, as many were, he was simply there to escape from the house for a couple of hours to himself and play cards games with his old cronies. He would happily make his half pint glass of Shandy last the whole evening long.

It was during these evenings when she had first arrived that Elsie would call up to Maria, inviting her downstairs. She hated the thought of her sat alone in her bedroom. Not knowing what horrific things she'd had to experience in her short twenty years of life, she wanted her to be aware that she was not alone. She wanted Maria to know that the kind of support and love her family had presumably given her back home, was available if she wanted it and ever needed it.

Elsie, with her kind heart, would sit them both down, making Maria feel comfortable in the warmth of the coal fire in the front Parlour, listening to the wireless or putting a vinyl on the record player. Elsie would make them both a cup of sweet tea or a mug of delicious hot chocolate, with which they would wash down a slice of freshly baked cake or biscuits that Elsie had busily prepared for them earlier in the day. Both enjoying the company each other provided, whilst it also gave the opportunity for a little tutoring lesson.

Elsie as well as Maria learning words of a new language.

Hanging Rosa's drenched coat over the old wooden clothes rail in the kitchen, she then placed the sodden shoes on the fire hearth to dry out and rushed eagerly upstairs to join the girls. "Is it safe for me to come in? Are you decent?" Elsie teased, as she reached Maria's doorway.

Maria and Rosa glanced at each other, puzzled looks on their faces in response.

"Please," Maria had answered, as she tightened the towelling housecoat around her body.

Often forgetting the barriers of language and understanding, she entered the small bedroom of floral papered walls.

Although Maria had been in Stockport for a short while now, the few good friends she had made, were also displaced persons, so with convenience they comfortably used their own language between them. There was little opportunity to try and use the English language, as they were often quite rudely avoided by the some of the local people; being disregarded as members of the community in their ignorance.

Rosa busily rummaged inside the 'communal handbag' and finally produced a beautiful, golden tube of lipstick. She had been carefully saving a small amount of her earnings for some weeks to buy this gift for Maria, convinced that today was certainly a day for such expensive luxuries.

Glancing at the lipstick Maria gleamed. This was something she had only ever seen in the magazine she flicked through in the canteen, during her lunch break at the mill.

A fellow worker Margaret had bought the magazine to work to show the other girls a pattern for a summer dress she was hoping to begin sewing. Maria was amazed to see how pretty a lady could look with this additional colour to her lips and felt for sure that wearing this product herself would make her feel like the most beautiful bride.

Rosa stood up from the edge of the bed where she had sat and leaning over, she placed the lipstick onto the obscure glass tray on the dressing table. Maria jumped up from the stool, pulling her friend towards her, she gave her a tight, loving thankyou hug.

As they embraced Elsie rushed from the room, realising that these young ladies had not come across makeup before and seeing their happiness had given her an idea. "One moment girls," she called as she left through the doorway.

As a woman in her late forties, Elsie didn't wear makeup very often, but she had done in the past, for special occasions, and she understood how it made a woman feel like a lady, even when it was applied lightly.

Returning just moments later, she carried in a small pink, satin purse and passed it to Maria to use as she wanted. "Help yourselves, both of you," she offered.

Trying to contain their young schoolgirl type giggles, they looked inside. In all her life, Maria had never seen beauty cosmetics and was quite unsure what went where and how on earth these items should be used. Rouge, lipstick, an eye liner, mascara, and a stunning glass bottle.

She removed the cute little golden lid and lifted the glass bottle up towards her nose. It contained the most delightful aroma, like a meadow of fresh flowers on a sunny day.

Elsie soon willingly took over the process of making Maria feel like the fairy-tale princess she was going to be today. Firstly, a dusting of pink rouge was brushed over her smooth youthful cheeks, giving her a warm glow. A little mascara lifted her stunning blue eyes. Elsie decided she didn't need any eye liner as her eyes were already naturally dark lined.

She passed the golden gift over to Rosa to make the finishing touches to the blushing bride to be. Opening the tube to reveal a stunning English rose pink lipstick.

"Piekny," exclaimed Rosa.

"Harnyy," agreed Maria, smiling. It certainly was beautiful.

Once the pale pink gloss had been placed along her lips Maria turned towards the mirror, smoothing her lips together, stunned into silence, she studied her face. She felt just as fantastic as she looked.

Staring into the mirror, sorrow washed over her as a sad thought suddenly rushed into her mind. If only her family back home could see her now, all grown up and entering a marriage to the man she loved with all her heart. Her eyes stung as she let a memory of her family surround her.

Her thoughts were suddenly snapped away from her as Elsie gently took her by the arm to stand, guiding her around the small bed to the wardrobe where a long ivory bag clung to a coat hanger on the open door.

Slowly, Maria gently unzipped the floor length bag to expose the magnificent silk, white wedding dress.

With very little space to manoeuvre in the small bedroom, Elsie suggested, "Shall I?" pointing towards the dress, wanting to help her into this graceful, delicate most exquisite gown.

"Please," responded Maria shyly. Presuming this was an offer of help, she removed the housecoat she wore, exposing her womanly, curvy body. Maria, keen to wear the white lace covered garment, ignored the hinted embarrassment of standing briefly in just her underwear.

Cautiously, she stepped into the layered white fabric. The fall of the satin shimmered as the long, classic dress was pulled up and onto her shoulders. She placed her arms into the long, voluminous sleeves, securing the arms into place with the tiny ivory buttons at the cuffs. A pattern of intricate ivory beads glistened around the waistline, lining the curves of Maria's body.

Once she had wriggled into place, Elsie carefully pulled up the zip at back, fastening the minute button around the neckline. Reaching around Maria, she gently picked up the large ivory headdress from the bed, allowing the long flowing veil to drape onto the floor.

She Brushed Maria's soft curls back from her face with her fingers and fixed the comb section of the band into place on the top of her head. Fluffing the veil around Maria's shoulders and framing the bride.

The dress fitted perfectly, perfection!

Maria felt incredible. As she turned around, so did Rosa. A hairbrush in her hand and her mouth gapping open in wonder as she glanced over at the bride.

"O moj, piekny dama," she cried.

Neither Maria nor Elsie understood these words, but both presumed it to be a compliment and the whole room smiled.

Maria strolled gracefully towards the wooden chair by the doorway. Carefully, she took a seat and watched as Elsie became the makeup lady once again, this time for Rosa.

A short time later, with both young ladies beaming with happiness and feeling amazing, Elsie quietly left the room to allow Rosa to dress without embarrassment.

Earlier in the week, she had brought to Elsie's house, a very smart looking pink woollen jacket and a matching knee-length skirt, accompanied with a cute white blouse. Her outfit would complement the bride and the bridal bouquet appropriately and thoughtfully.

Elsie, had been purposely dressed and readily available for several hours, wanting to spend the time prior to the ceremony supporting Maria in any way that was required. She hurried along in her usual way, down the stairs and into the small, dingy kitchen to the rear of her home.

Peering out through the window, she could see with relief that the miserable weather had at least calmed. The last of the vicious rain seemed to be slowly dripping away.

On the kitchen countertop sat the four golden rimmed wine glasses. She had polished and set them out earlier in the day.

She pulled open the larder door and removed the bottle of sparkling wine that she'd lavishly bought for this special occasion. Neither Sid nor herself were particularly great drinkers, and she doubted the girls were experienced with alcohol either, but she felt it was a necessity, as a little toast to the day ahead and a bit of a nerve settler; for herself as much as for anyone else. Her nerves were shot. She hadn't felt this nervous since her own wedding day to Sid, back in 1927.

Although today, her nerves were for Maria and her future. So much about Maria and her previous life was still unknown to them, unspoken, but Elsie could see how much she had relaxed in recent months. More of her delightful singing was taking place than ever before, they had noted.

That could only mean one thing.

Happiness.

Sid and Elsie had only met Myroslaw (or Slawko as Maria had lovingly called him of late), on a few occasions.

At twenty-five he was a few years older than Maria. Although the smart young man appeared to be very honest and reliable, with an obvious caring nature, they both couldn't help but worry.

Had this whirlwind romance moved too quickly?

Maria had only known Myroslaw for eight months. Did she really know him well enough to gift him the lifelong commitment of marriage?

However, they both seemed totally smitten and it was obvious they had given each other a huge sense of security and normality. This alone had to be a good thing.

Elsie often had to remind herself that they weren't Maria's parents, although they had become extremely fond of her during her stay with them. They were immensely proud of this kind and thoughtful addition to their lives; they only wanted the very best that life could offer her.

If they had been formally asked for their blessing, it would have been given in a flash.

Hearing Sid saunter along the hallway towards the kitchen, she turned around. Looking every bit the gentleman that he had always been, dressed in a neat grey suit and crisp white shirt; Elsie's breath caught.

She'd always thought he looked handsome in a suit, although he had aged some since their own wedding day and the opportunity for wearing such attire was infrequent, just the odd funeral or wedding to attend.

Elsie had chosen him a pale grey tie to complete the smart look and once she had adjusted it neatly around his collar, they both carried the glasses and the tall bottle of fizz through to the parlour.

Always a stippler for keeping to time, Elsie glanced at the clock sitting central on the mantlepiece. It showed quarter past two. Noting the minutes marching away from them, she called up the stairs, from the hallway, for the girls to come down. Feeling the need for a few moments to calm down a house full of nerves and excitement. Her own nerves especially.

Maria looked stunning as she gracefully stepped down the staircase, taking care of the swift layers of smooth satin mopping the floor as she moved. The beautiful soft, white veil gave her extra height on her petite five-foot-two-inch stature.

All focus fixed on her, as both Elsie and Sid stood quietly rooted, with tears of pride welling up in their eyes. If only her parents could see their daughter now, they both thought.

After a short toast and a few sips of bubbles, last-minute touch ups of lipstick were applied and hair styling was completed.

Gently, Rosa passed Maria her bridal bouquet, quite a simple but effectively stunning floral spray, releasing the sweetest fragrance. The white carnations picked out the purity of the lace within her dress and pretty, pink roses sang of the vibrancy of living. As beautiful and meaningful as the roses received at their first date. Long trails of greenery and swirled ivory ribbons draped thoughtfully around the arrangement in simplicity.

Sid had parked his car at the front of the house, ready to take the four of them to the church. He had previously moaned to Elsie that it was a ridiculous journey to make in a car, it would literally take them longer to all get into the car than the actual the travelling time, he had grumbled. Elsie, as usual had got her own way after arguing that no bride should have to walk to church for her own wedding. As the weather looked so unpredictable for the rest of the day, Sid, for once tended to agree.

Maria ruched up her dress slightly, allowing her to sit in the back of the car. The excitement of the morning preparations had distracted her from imagining how her wedding back home would have taken form.

As she stared out of the window, an image of the village lane came into her thoughts. A glimmer of herself and Myroslaw leaving her family home, making their way to the church. Her parents gently throwing a sprinkling of holy water their way as the journey began. The bright, colourful procession of cheerful musicians. Family and guests lining the lane, singing songs as they walk along to the church. The bride and groom enter the church together, as willing and equal partners.

At three o'clock sharp, the little blue Morris Minor pulled up outside Our Lady's Roman Catholic Church, a grand looking gothic building. Two pinnacle towers rose up high above the huge, round, stained-glass flower-patterned window. The bells chiming from the tower above, loud, and magnificent, an announcement to be heard all over town. Stepping out from the car, Elsie gave Maria a gentle squeeze on her arm, placing a loving kiss on her cheek.

"Good luck beautiful, be happy," she whispered into her ear.

Walking ahead of the girls and passing the shrub filled gardens on the lead up to the entrance, Elsie linked her arm lovingly through Sid's and entered the church through one of the two enormous, gothic arched doorways.

The groom stood suited and calm, just inside the church, the camp's Ukrainian priest dressed in his floor length cassock at his side. Both patiently awaited Maria's entrance.

Elsie beamed with happiness. It was wonderful to see that many of Maria's fellow mill workers, both the locals and the latest workers arriving from overseas, had come to support Maria on her big day.

A pleasant surprise to also see that a hand full of neighbours, having taken a liking to Maria; the newest resident on the street, had kindly joined the ceremony to offer the bride and groom their very best of wishes.

Marriage of Maria & Myroslaw

Our Lady's Catholic Church, Stockport

With the added addition of several nosey parishioners and community do-gooders who wanted to take a look at a Ukrainian marriage ceremony; it made the huge church seem a little warmer and slightly less sparse.

Taking their seats on the front pew, with Sid close beside her, Elsie glanced around. At the front of the aisle stood a young gentleman, she understood this was Myroslaw's good friend Ivan Lypnij. Both the groom and Ivan looking like they had stepped off a movie set, with their good looks, slicked back hair and sharp looking suits.

Behind Mr Lipnij, a couple of rows were filled with smart looking guests, mainly men, but some with women by their sides. Elsie presumed these to be from Myroslaw's camp and was grateful that, they too, had made the journey on this special occasion.

Elsie couldn't help but feel a dreadful sadness that there wasn't a blood relative to be seen. If they had survived the dreadful war, wherever they were, sadly, they were totally unaware of this beautiful and very special occasion.

As the chimes settled, Maria and Rosa made their way into the church entrance.

Myroslaw, standing tall and proud, smiled, his breath taken away by this beauty in white, approaching him. He still felt a rush of excitement when he saw Maria, just like he had the first day he had set eyes on her, he felt the luckiest man alive. His eyes welled up with tears of pride, to have this strong, beautiful woman by his side.

Having spent the last few years thankful to be alive, he was now thankful for the opportunity to spend the rest of his life with Maria. She made him so happy. Life was going to be good with her by his side.

Taking her man's side, Maria shared in his proud smile, feeling for sure that life was going to be good if they shared it together.

She believed you should follow your heart, a path that she was about to take throughout her married life.

Blessing the wedding bands, the priest then took hold of Maria's right hand, placing the ring onto her fourth finger before he turned to Myroslaw and repeated the procedure. A belief that this finger has a vein directly connecting it to the heart, 'the vein of love'.

Presenting each of them with a burning candle, he then took their free hand and lead them down to the front of the altar.

The Ukrainian ceremony began.

Rosa headed off, scattering a light shower of pink rose petals to the ground, a beautiful pathway for the bride to tread upon, down to the front of the aisle as she joined Elsie and Sid.

Psalm 127 began to echo around the walls, as the couple followed the priest along the aisle. Each of them carried before them a tall candle, lit as a reminder that Christ is 'the light of the world', a symbol of joy and warmth.

The hands of the couple were joined with an embroidered rushnyk cloth. They remained bound throughout the ceremony to signify their union.

They had been unable to follow a great many of their own traditions on the run up to the wedding, but the opportunity to have this Ukrainian ceremony had meant the world to them both. They were immensely grateful for the efforts of the priest from The Heath Camp and the church for allowing such a wedding and making it all possible. The congregation enjoyed the beautiful hymns and, although only a dozen or so Ukrainian speakers sang, the sound was still intense and beautifully sung.

After the final blessing, the ceremony came to an end and a loving kiss meaningfully sealed their marriage. The newlywed couple happily breezed out of the church into the world as husband and wife.

This marriage had been one of the first Ukrainian weddings to take place in Stockport. Although the Ukrainian Priest had permission to conduct and officiate the wedding, as there were no Ukrainian Churches, the ceremony had taken place in an English-speaking Catholic church.

Therefore, the couple still needed to sign the registry certificate.

Sid drove the happy couple and their witnesses the short journey to the Registrar Office and once the witnesses, Elsie and Ivan, had signed the register, their journey to a life side by side began.

Myroslaw and Ivan had stayed the evening before in the Bluebell Hotel and the owners, having gotten to know Myroslaw quite well from his previous stays, had kindly agreed to hold a small gathering in the bar area after the marriage ceremony. Around twenty-five guests attended; Elsie had generously paid the hotel landlord to serve some small sandwiches at the reception.

Nadia and Iryna, two wives from the camp whom Maria had met previously, had been busy baking the wedding gift from The Heath Camp community.

Once they had managed to source the main ingredients, it had been their absolute pleasure to bake something so meaningful. It brought back memories of happier days when they too were married back in their homeland. They were grateful to have found their husbands and be back in their lives, some women they knew hadn't been as lucky.

They thoughtfully presented the couple with a 'Korovai,' a traditional Ukrainian wedding bread. A large, round braided sweet bread, baked using wheat flour. A symbol of good luck and prosperity. Symbolically decorated with two doves, made from dough to represent the couple and other birds to represent friends and family. The whole bread was surrounded by a wreath of greenery, a symbol of love and purity.

The couple were amazed at such a kind and thoughtful gesture. As Myroslaw headed towards the hotel's kitchen area in search of a knife to cut into the bread, Maria waited in the doorway, placing the gift onto a side table.

She took a moment for herself, glancing around the small room. Taking in the relaxed and happy faces dotted around the tables, sharing conversations and laughter as they grazed their way through the delicious sandwiches, she smiled to herself. *All these special people, how lucky are we to have them in our lives.*

Myroslaw returned, holding the knife, his new wife waiting patiently in the doorway to greet him with a kiss. Maria was bubbling with happiness; her huge smile proved as much to him.

It had been a truly amazing day. A day he didn't want to ruin with his worries, but with so many running around in his head, he struggled to place them to the back of his thoughts. He had wanted nothing more than to marry Maria but leaving the camp and being in a position to find a new job hadn't proved to be as easy and straight-forward as he had originally thought.

There were so many official forms to fill in, each of them took weeks for a reply and often came with another form to fill in. He was grateful to the camp officer who helped him to complete the forms, that had annoyingly arrived in English. Maybe a couple of drinks would help ease his anxieties.

Cutting into the lightly baked bread, Maria soon began wondering around the tables, sharing the gift between their guests. Myroslaw headed over to his camp friends.

Ivan was staying for just a few hours, as were his fellow campmates, before travelling back to Wellingore on the late-night bus. He headed to the bar to buy a couple of bottles of vodka and request some small shot glasses for the table.

There had been very little to celebrate in recent years, now though, they were thankful for this day. It was a day filled with happiness. It was certainly a time to celebrate, and Ukrainians know only too well how to celebrate hard and most definitely celebrate in style.

Returning to the table with the celebratory drinks, he began to pour and share the offerings around to the other guests.

Ivan stood tall, a small shot glass of vodka in hand. "Kozhen, kozhen," he repeated loudly to gather everyone's attention.

The room became quiet as the guests turned to face the couple who had gathered beside Ivan.

Raising the glass to toast the happy couple, Ivan announced, "Myroslaw and Maria, Nazdarovya," wishing them both a cheers and good health.

"Nazdarovya," he repeated towards the guests, before again raising his glass and pouring the neat vodka into his mouth.

"Nazdarovya," the room returned in an echoed reply.

Empty glasses soon clattered down on the tables.

The wedding celebrations had begun.

A few of Maria's co-workers had come to help them celebrate. They had kindly joined together and bought a beautiful, tall glass vase as a wedding gift for the happy couple. Wrapped up in a tough, brown packaging paper, they had fastened a beautiful large yellow ribbon around it. Hugs and kisses were exchanged between the colleagues as the gift was gratefully received.

Several of the neighbours too, had called in to the hotel reception bringing with them their best wishes and kind thoughts for the new couple. As well as many beautiful gifts between them.

The newlyweds were extremely thankful, feeling totally welcomed into the neighbourhood, if a little overwhelmed by the kindness and generosity shown.

With both communities respectful of the other, mixing so well, the evening was full of laughter. A sudden and surprise appearance of a mandolin from a neighbour caused excitement. The wedding party soon erupted as a lively folk singing was led by Maria and dancing filled the small dance area in the room. A new experience for the English guests and a feeling of home for the Ukrainians.

It was a perfect ending to this special day.

As the party of guests reluctantly left for home. Maria and Myroslaw retired to their hotel room to spend their first night together as Mr and Mrs Myron.

3
Setting Up A Life Together

The next morning, following a heavy feast of fresh fried eggs and bacon for breakfast, the newlyweds reluctantly left the pleasantness of the hotel. It had been a wonderful twenty-four hours and they both felt upbeat about their future life together.

Empty clouds fluttered in the sky above. The morning air felt crisp and fresh. Hand in hand they breezed along the paved cobbles heading towards Worral Street.

The previous day had been the happiest day Myroslaw could remember.

Despite Maria's calm approach to beginning married life, she could sense Myroslaw was brooding about the coming weeks. She had spent the last few months thinking about the wedding arrangements and hadn't given much thought to how life would be once they were actually wed. Planning ahead had never really been something she needed to do. Life had just happened.

She gently squeezed his hand in hers, leaning in towards him, she rested her head on his shoulders.

"Vse, bude dobre." She smiled as she caught his eyes in hers, assuring him all will be good.

Elsie had kept a keen look out for the happy pair to arrive. It would be an uncomfortable squeeze for them to be sharing the small bedroom and Elsie was concerned how the dynamics of the household would work now with an extra resident, a male too. She hoped she wouldn't need to be setting out extra house rules for the young couple. They would have to take each day as it came, she supposed.

Elsie, as landlady of the house, had purposely held off informing the Ministry of Labour Office, aware that Maria's contract dated 21st November 1947 was coming to an end. She expected they would soon be receiving a visit from Mrs Chamberlain once she had been informed of the marriage.

She had recently taken the signed contract, from out of the old oak bureau that stood, highly polished, in the corner of the parlour. Confirming her thoughts as she read, it stated that Maria could only stay in the lodgings as a single woman. Concerned, Elsie hastened to think what this may mean for Maria and her employment. She hadn't wanted to mention these worries to Maria and spoil the excitement of the wedding, but she realised it would need to be discussed shortly.

The Westward Ho scheme had many stipulations, and she prayed this rather quick marriage wouldn't ruin all the months of settling that had taken place for the pair.

***

Although Elsie and Sid had been very accommodating to begin with, starting a married life in a cramped one room lodging wasn't proving to be the easiest.

Maria had been kept on the Westward Ho scheme. As she was now a married woman, the stay at the lodgings had been kindly offered temporarily by Elsie, 'Until they had two incomes coming in and were able to find suitable housing for themselves.'

Possibly because of the move, Myroslaw had begun to have extremely unsettled sleep, disturbed by horrendous nightmares. Something that had settled slightly in recent months, but had reared its nasty head once more.

Waking in the small bedroom each night in a state of cold sweat and uncontrollable shaking, it obviously had an effect on Maria too.

These suppressed memories being unleashed, although terribly painful and unbelievably mind shattering as they were, surely needed to be shared with someone trustworthy. Maria was his wife, his support. She wanted so much to help her husband with these demons. She thought it might even give her the strength and courage to also share her own nightmares.

How could they even begin to divulge such harrowing details?

Myroslaw had reluctantly returned to visit the Heath Camp a couple of times since their wedding. Each time, it had been for an official appointment with the camp officer.

Although his marriage and leave had been approved, there were various documents that needed signing. These would allow him to leave the camp officially and permanently and hopefully allow him take up employment.

Myroslaw was determined to find work whilst awaiting official leave from the camp. Rising early each morning to wash and shave. Appearance was an importance to him. Standing in front of the mirror in the bedroom he shared with Maria, he brushed his hand over the shoulder of his suit jacket, checking his collar was neat.

"Today's the day!" he convinced himself. Feeling positive as he set out to pay a call on the local businesses to offer his willing employment.

A little over two months later, on 21st January 1949, the official army discharge documents were delivered by post. Myroslaw could finally begin work at Portwood Spinning Company, a job that he had secured several weeks earlier, following his excessive weeks of hunting.

Myroslaw had been keen to start work and provide for his new wife. Being a hardworking man, he wasn't fazed by the long days, sometimes working quite late into the evening. However, this meant he would often miss the last bus into Stockport town centre.

Working long hours and having a lengthy walk back to the lodgings at the end of his shifts, Myroslaw was soon feeling exhausted.

Although Maria worried this would be too much for him with the lack of sleep, it was thankfully just the help he needed to put him into a deep sleep at night, easing the daily nightmares.

Their lives unfortunately were a repeated pattern of work and sleep, with little time spent as a couple.

Maria became frustrated that she didn't have the opportunity to be the great wife she would prove to be. She wanted to be able to cook for her husband, lovingly make him the Ukrainian dishes she had made for her brothers so often back in their homeland.

However, with Elsie having already cooked and served her man's meal earlier in the evening, as Maria was arriving home from work, she felt it an inconvenience to start cooking so late and messing up the kitchen after Elsie's pots had been tidied away. Elsie didn't offer the use of the kitchen, so she presumed it wasn't an option.

With Elsie and Sid relaxing comfortably in the parlour after their evening meal, Maria would sit in her bedroom and await Myroslaws return. Sadly, he was often so tired, they would both just eat a sandwich or slice of cold pie and sleep the night away.

They trundled on through the cold winter months, spending any free time at the weekends, wrapped up warm, going for walks through the local park or meeting up with a few newfound friends. Fellow Ukrainians, that also found themselves beginning a life in Stockport. They loved the company and appreciated the support knowing that, they too, shared a similar harrowing past and an uncertain future.

The British community didn't understand the complexes of Eastern European politics. This was a topic that could only be shared between themselves. It was usually the men that would spend long hours discussing such things.

As Spring arrived, Maria suggested that maybe they could find new lodgings, somewhere closer to Myroslaws employment. As his work shifts were the longest, it made sense to cut down on the journey home at the end of the day.

One of their new friends in Edgeley had heard about a room for rent in Bredbury. Neither Maria nor Myroslaw knew the area at the other side of Stockport particularly well, but as it was closer to Vernon Mill where Myroslaw worked and they had heard there were a couple of Ukrainians in the area too, it all seemed to be good move.

With all the relevant paperwork for Mrs Chamberlain completed, informing the labour office of her new address on 28th May 1949, the couple packed up their few belongings and bid a farewell to the landlords and neighbours of Worral Street. There was a mixture of emotions all around and promises that they'd all stay in touch.

Rosa, who hadn't seen much of Maria in recent months, also came to wish them both the best of luck in their new home, bringing with her a homemade Victoria sponge cake as a housewarming gift.

They soon settled into their new lodgings. A small two-bedroom terraced house. Its dining room to the back of the house had been converted into a bedroom. This single room, with gaudy patterned wallcoverings, was to be the new home for the couple.

Maria soon discovered a huge benefit to the move; she noticed that the husband and wife landlords were quite often out until late into the evenings. This gave her the opportunity after her day at the Mill to spend time in the kitchen. The lady of the house wasn't house proud to say the least, not like Elsie had been. Much to her annoyance, Maria would often have to scrub the kitchen clean before she could even begin cooking.

She would make enough food for the next couple of evenings, sometimes with the help of Rosa, who, missing her friend, would take a detour after work to call for a quick catch up with Maria, before Myroslaw returned home from work.

Returning home from a long late shift to find the most delicious dish of potato dumpling 'Vereniki,' offerings, cabbage and meat parcels 'Holubshi,' or a bowl of hot beetroot 'Borsch' soup, was definitely the way to her man's heart. It was a refreshing change for them to be able to sit at the small wooden dining table in the kitchen and share a meal together, a chance to discuss how their day had gone. They were beginning to become a normal young married couple.

Over the glorious, hot summer months, they spent much of their free time socialising with their new Ukrainian friends, giving them an opportunity to get out of their room and leave the routine of work, work, work behind for the day.

Mostly, they would meet up locally at Vernon Park. Each of the friends would take with them and share out any food they could lay their hands on. Spreading out a blanket on the grass, they would enjoy a picnic together. Seemingly there were more people added to their group gathering each week, as word got around of fellow Ukrainians in Stockport.

These gatherings became a great network of support to each of them, they had the feeling of a real family unit. Each of them nurtured and preserved a deep cultural and religious tie with their homeland, some 2000 miles away.

The women sat happily and chatted together endlessly for hours. Maria was in her element speaking about their lives in Stockport, their jobs and new homes, but also, they spoke about their families back in their homeland. This often caused upset amongst them. It was the not knowing that saddened them. So many unanswered questions nagged at their minds.

Had their families survived?

Did they still have a home to return to in Ukraine?

Would they be able to return to their homeland one day?

Would it ever be safe to do so?

While the women huddled deep within their chatter, the men discussed their work life, their life in England, their lives back in their homeland, a life they missed so dearly, a country they held deep in their hearts.

Each of them knew they would probably never be able, or even dare, to return home for fear of reprisal and persecution. Terrified of the thought of what would happen to them if they attempted to go back, discussions would tend to become heated.

Each of the men had such strong, vivid political views on the mistreatment they had suffered, what their country had endured. They grieved for what they had lost, while the torture still churned deep inside them, causing fresh knots to twist in their stomachs with every thought.

Remembering vividly the daily struggle for survival on the concentration camps that Myroslaw amongst others in the group had encountered. Regular beatings, raw and brutal. The exhaustion felt from the forced labour that had been required from them, whilst suffering an inhumane starvation. The men witnessed and experienced horrendous pain inflicted on the prisoners. The camp guards showed no remorse or conscience and sometimes even had a look of pleasure as they delivered this extreme violence.

It was during those beautiful summer months, just a couple of months since moving into the new lodgings, that Maria discovered she was pregnant. Even though they were both totally delighted to be creating a family of their own, it was also quite a worrying time. The thought of bringing a new baby into such a small, cramped bedroom, and into a house that wasn't kept the cleanest, even with Maria's enormous efforts, was quite a concerning time.

The icy cold months of winter arrived, along with the unexpected news from the landlords, that they would not be allowing a baby at the lodgings. Maria's pregnancy had recently become quite obvious as she bloomed. They hadn't deliberately concealed the news, but neither had either of them shouted it from the rooftops, unsure of the situation they might find themselves in.

Once again, they were soon packing up their few possessions and moving to a new lodging at the other side of Stockport.

With just three months left until the baby was due and suddenly feeling most unwelcome, they hastily moved into Kingsland Road, Cheadle Heath.

Maria felt satisfied, knowing that the Landlords were in agreement to them welcoming a baby into the house in the near future.

Myroslaw had called to the house to view and secure the room, during the previous week, so Maria was longing to see it for herself. She was pleasantly surprised as they arrived at the front door of the attractive semi-detached house, that stood on a quiet cobbled road. Upstairs, the three reasonably sized bedrooms housed two other sets of lodgers besides the room they had taken. Downstairs the dining room to the side of the small drab kitchen was used as the bedroom for the landlords. To the front of the house, a parlour was laid out with two threadbare armchairs and a sofa, covered with a large grey throw.

The house was clean and tidy by Maria's standards, but she couldn't help but notice the lack of comfort. The walls were bare of any paintings, there were no ornaments, no soft furnishings. Nothing to make this stark house feel like a home.

They attempted to settle into a new routine. Maria informed her employers of her pregnancy. Unfortunately, they were not going to be holding her position open for her to return to once the baby had arrived.

Maria was unsure how they would manage with just one wage coming in, especially when they would have an extra mouth to feed shortly. She also didn't know who would take care of the baby so she could go to work. Having no family around to help them was proving difficult for the pair. Although, they had made some wonderful friends who, of course, shared the excitement of the new addition that was due, they too were having their own struggles in one way or another. Life in general wasn't easy for any of them, no matter how hard they all worked.

***

During the next few months, Maria found that her ever growing pregnancy bump made it difficult to manoeuvre the machinery at the mill. It had been heavy and bulky enough to use before her pregnancy. She continued to tell herself that at least she had money coming in whilst she could, hoping with each pay packet that she could manage to put a little to one side for when they needed it most. But with the new-born's arrival quickly nearing, there were baby items to gather.

One warm, spring evening, Rosa had surprised her friend by meeting her outside the mill after a long, tiring shift. Rosa had noticed on a visit the previous week that her friend was looking exhausted, and she wanted to help the mother-to-be in some way.

Together, they steadily walked through the back streets of Stockport and down towards the new lodgings, a daily walk that had been taking a toll on Maria lately.

Glad to be returning home, her sore, blistered feet would swell to match her swollen ankles.

Thankfully, the lodgings were usually empty of other residents early evening. Mr Barnes, a single young man who lived in the bedroom opposite their room, worked night shifts and had often left the house before Maria returned home. The other bedroom to the side of Maria and Myroslaws was home to an older man, known simply to the couple as Tom. Maria heard more from Tom than she actually saw of him, usually in the late hours of the night, as he stumbled drunkenly into his bed. He was a regular drinker, spending most evening in the public houses around Stockport, heading directly to the boozer from work. Maria wondered how he managed to wake each morning and complete a day at work. The landlords of the lodgings also ran a bakery. They worked long hours and were barely seen in the house.

It was quite peaceful at this time of the evening. A relieved Maria sat on the sofa in the front room for a few minutes to take the weight off her feet before preparing their evening meal.

Rosa made her comfortable with the soft cushions that she propped behind her and carefully carried the brown paper bag she had brought with her out into the kitchen. She quickly busied herself making a pot of tea and placed the two chocolate éclair cream cakes she had brought onto a plate. A lovely treat for them both.

Returning to the front room to see a weary Maria had put her feet up on the sofa and had closed her eyes with exhaustion, Rosa gently placed the tea tray down on the table so as not to disturb this rare moment of rest. She had never known Maria to rest. She was always on the go, with something or other to get done.

As she poured the tea Maria opened her eyes and smiled. Five minutes relaxing had made all the difference and a cup of hot tea would taste even better, having been freshly made by a good, caring friend.

Once the pair had swilled down the tasty cake treat with their cups of tea, Rosa poured another for Maria, insisting her expectant friend stayed in her comfortable state on the sofa whilst she had the chance to rest.

"Stay," she ordered, pleased with herself, for having learned a useful new English word.

Returning to the kitchen, Rosa peeped into the small corner pantry. The shelves were labelled with each of the tenant's names, this made the task ahead much easier. On Maria's shelf she obviously found plenty of potatoes and onions. This gave her an idea.

She had recently watched her own landlady cooking what she had called 'Hotpot' and as she could also see a handful of carrots and a tin of corned beef, she set about peeling the potatoes and making an evening meal for her friends.

Once the ingredients were bubbling away and a delicious aroma began filling the room, she added the beef stock into the stew. She turned down the heat on the stove to a simmer, pleased with herself that she could return some of the goodness that Maria had lavished on her by just being her friend. She carefully sliced off a couple of chunks from the bread she found in the pantry. Myroslaw would be hungry when he returned from his shift.

Back in the front room Maria, appreciating the help but feeling guilty for taking time out, sat up on the sofa, her tired feet still dreadfully swollen, but the throbbing blisters had at least eased slightly. The half hour rest had done her the world of good. She was so lucky to have Rosa as her best friend, forever kind and thoughtful.

The swollen feet and the walk to the mill continued for the next few weeks, keen to keep earning money for as long as she could, while she could.

With just days to go until Maria's due date, her last shift had arrived. Although the working day was just like any other, hot, dusty and noisy, the lunch break in the canteen was anything but the usual. Maria's workmates made a massive fuss of her. A couple of them brought in homemade cakes, one had made a delicious, double layered, chocolate cake and another had made a tangy lemon cake, drizzled in lashings of tasty icing sugar. It seemed everyone was excited as they gathered around to present gifts to the mother-to-be.

A cute lemon cardigan had been patiently knitted, along with a tiny white bonnet and a pair of booties. A few of the ladies had kindly collected money between them and bought a set of two crisp, white bedding sheets. for the crib. The final gift to be opened was a chunky crocheted blanket in the softest lemon and white wool.

Tears rolled silently down Maria's cheeks. She wasn't usually one to cry or particularly show her emotions, but she couldn't contain her weeping. She was honoured to have been treated so well and touched that these ladies would spend their precious time and money on her and her baby. It meant the world to her to know she had such good people by her side.

Just a few days later, on 28th April, Maria gave birth to a beautiful, dark-haired, healthy baby girl. The young couple were overjoyed to become parents. They lovingly named their new daughter Olha, meaning 'Holy.'

A week-long stay at Stepping Hill Hospital followed the labour, Maria found she was a natural at motherhood and although the staff were kind and supportive, it was a struggle to spend so much time with another dialect, a language she still didn't understand very well. Thankfully, Myroslaw was able to make the bus journey to the hospital each evening once his shift had finished, to visit his wife and new-born daughter, brightening up all their days.

As a new little family unit, they soon settled into a routine. Maria thoroughly enjoyed motherhood. She loved cuddling and taking care of this little bundle and, with the entrance of warmer weather, she was happy to take Olha out for a stroll in the pram they had bought from a neighbour. Proudly pushing the baby through the streets, as all new mothers do, showing off the baby to any passers-by and neighbours.

It was around this time that they received a surprise letter from Birmingham. Myroslaw's cousin Mykhailo had written asking for him to confirm if this was Myroslaw from the village of Halych. He had been in touch with the Red Cross Charity and asked for their help to search for any relatives that may have survived the war and arrived in Britain. He was particularly hopeful in finding the whereabouts of his favourite cousin.

Both Maria and Myroslaw had themselves written letters to their family back home, although neither had received a response yet, leaving them both anxious for news on the survival of family members.

Therefore, this was a huge boost for Myroslaw. With the help of their housemate, Mr Barnes, he had contacted the Red Cross himself, as had Maria since their arrival, with no luck in tracing any kin, so he was thrilled to find out that he had family in Britain. Suddenly, he felt a blanket of security wrapping around him, just knowing someone who shared his blood was within his reach. He had found life quite stressful in recent months. Although he put on a strong front for Maria, he felt exhausted trying to work enough hours to provide for his little family.

Myroslaw was the second eldest of seven boys born to Karolina. His mother had gone on to have the youngest five sons with her new husband after Myroslaws young father Ilya, had passed away suffering with gangrene.

His stepfather didn't have much time, let alone love for his stepchildren. Myroslaw had always been close to his cousin's family, the family of his father's brother. Especially Mikhailo, who, just eight years older than him, was closest in age, but old enough to be seen as a big brother.

They were good people. Both Mikhailo and his older sister Anna had encouraged him to attend school lessons and to get a good education. They had provided Myroslaw with financial support for his schooling during his teenage years. This was something his stepfather thought was a waste of time. He said Myroslaw should be working on the land like his brothers. He thought his studying was giving him too many big ideas, giving him too much to say. This caused huge fights to erupt between the two. Myroslaw had become immune to his stepfather's fist. He'd received many a beating over the years from the strict man his mother had, in his eyes, mistakenly married. Nothing would prevent him from his studies. There was much to learn about the politics of Ukraine, and he was going to learn it, with or without his stepfather's blessing.

* * *

Once he had shared the news with Maria, Myroslaw immediately raced to the nearby public phone box, just a few streets away. Nervously, he fumbled in his jacket pocket for some loose change and dialled the phone number in the letter. The phone call was soon answered, and he began chatting away to his long-lost cousin. It was a conversation full of emotion. Great happiness at being re-connected, with so much happier news for Myroslaw to share, but sadness in the knowledge of what they had both been through before arriving in Britain.

The following weekend, Mykhailo made the train journey to Stockport. He was delighted to see Myroslaw again and to meet his lovely wife and his beautiful baby daughter. It was several years since they had last seen each other at the start of the war. They had a huge amount of catching up to do.

Mykhailo stayed in Stockport for the weekend and spent the following day with Myroslaw, just the two of them, pacing the streets of Cheadle Heath from early morning. A much-needed opportunity for them both to talk in private and share their experiences, as frightening as it was.

They trusted each other with their lives.

Although it proved difficult to unleash the haunting times that they both tried so hard to bury, it helped them to deal with some of the traumas and Myroslaw was grateful for the opportunity to release some tension and anxiety, just the type of therapy he needed.

Maria was a wonderful wife and caring listener, but it was his role to be a stable, supportive husband. Although she quizzed him, he didn't want to burden her with too many details. He wasn't sure he was brave enough to discuss how he came about receiving the scars on his body or why he had received the tattooed numbers on his shoulder during his time held at Auschwitz concentration camp, for that matter. He didn't want her to see him for anything but the strong man that stood beside her. A time would come when their pasts would be shared, exposed to each other. For now, it could only be released piece by piece.

These visits became regular and the support from Mykhailo was always a pleasant occurrence.

In addition to this newly discovered support, there was also another wonderful person about to enter their lives and become a permanent fixture within their small family.

Myroslaw continued to work at Portwood Spinning Company. He was a likeable co-worker to have around, always a really hard worker and who could be relied upon. Even though Myroslaw worked long shifts, he was always willing to take on any extra hours to boost his pay slip at the end of the week. This pleased his fellow workers, as it made their working days a little easier, but it also impressed the management.

There were always time limits and orders to get ready and his supervisor, Elsie Jowett, was impressed by Myroslaws work ethics. She had been Myroslaws supervisor since his first day arriving at the company in 1948. With Myroslaw speaking no English at all at this stage, Elsie took him under her wing. He always seemed totally respectful, eager to please and fit in at the workplace.

She gave him the opportunity to prove his worth in his actions and this he more than did. Unsure of Myroslaw's background, she could tell he was well educated. He seemed to have an intellect that made her wonder if he would be better suited to a higher-level position, once his language skills had improved. Knowing he had come to Stockport from a labour camp as a prisoner of war, she could only imagine the cruelty and the horrendous times he had experienced prior to this.

Seeing on his records that he was married and had obviously settled well in Stockport, she noticed on the odd occasion his small, lovely looking, wife met him outside the mill at lunchtime. She pushed a clean but very old pram along and brought with her a sandwich for her husband.

Elsie was impressed, but she couldn't quite understand how both Myroslaw and his wife looked so clean and smart, when she knew how much Myroslaw earned and how they lived in quite poor conditions. This wasn't a look she was used to seeing.

Since she had arrived from Uppermill after her divorce some ten years previous, she had never met a smarter looking mill worker. She was most impressed by how this young couple kept themselves looking the best they could and kept the baby spotlessly clean and neat.

Elsie, at fifty-years-old, was back living in Stockport with her elderly parents. Sadly, she had never been able to have children, unsure if the medical reason was with herself or her ex-husband and his heavy drinking.

Elsie and her parents were never short of time or money. She was eager to help this beautiful little family in any way she possibly could.

And so, the relationship began, and she became part of all their lives, part of their family.

'Auntie Elsie,' she was proudly named outside of the Mill.

Keen to have Olha christened as soon as possible, the couple had arranged for the priest from Heath camp to call at their lodgings to conduct a blessing on their new baby. They asked cousin Mykhailo if he would be the Godfather to Olha. Of course, he was hugely honoured to have been asked and assured the couple he would be more than happy to take on the responsibility.

The day of the Christening arrived, unfortunately the train Mykhailo was due to travel on from Birmingham was running late and he was therefore too late to take part in the ceremony. Rushing to fill this important position, Myroslaw asked a neighbouring Ukrainian, Mr Usick, if he would step in. Only too happy to help a friend and be asked such a request, he happily agreed.

The couple also invited a few of their good friends from the camp to join the journey with the priest, so it was an obvious choice to have one of the wives of the campmates as the Godmother. Both wanted Ukrainians to take on this important honour, knowing they shared the same beliefs as themselves.

It was a small affair with just their previous landlords, Elsie and Sid, attending and, of course, Rosa and Auntie Elsie also joined them. Following the simple service at their home, the guests tucked into the sandwiches Maria had prepared as she handed out endless cups of hot tea. The landlords allowed them to use the front room for a just couple of hours. It was a lovely gathering and a welcome change from the usual routine of the days.

Olha was mostly a happy baby during the day, eating well and settling easily for a nap in the afternoons. However, night times were a dreadfully, tiring time. Maria had tried all sorts, but she just couldn't settle her baby. Aware that the baby's crying disturbed the whole household had made an anxious Maria concerned. She would try to feed her extra before putting her down for the night, try to soothe her by lulling and rocking her, humming her beautiful songs.

Nothing worked!

Maybe it was the constant shutting of doors from the other lodger's and the landlords coming and going. Maybe it was the small, cramped, stuffy bedroom. Maybe the baby picked up on Maria's anxieties.

Whatever the reason, it soon became clear that they had outstayed their welcome at the lodgings.

One tiring morning following a very disturbed, unsettled night, Maria was in the kitchen making herself a strong cup of tea. The landlady stomped along the hallway, entering the room she immediately began shouting at Maria, close to her face.

"You must leave, we cannot have all this crying, the baby never stops, we all need our sleep, you must go, find somewhere else to live," she ranted angrily without taking a breath, her red face scowling at Maria.

Unsure what exactly was being screamed towards her, Maria was upset and presumed it could only be the crying baby that was causing the problem.

Stunned into silence, she didn't know how to reply. Tired and feeling emotional herself, she could feel tears springing into her eyes. Speechless, she left the unfinished cup of tea on the drainer and walked from the room.

Returning to their bedroom, she quietly closed the door behind her. She walked over to the bed and sat down, holding her head in her hands. She felt like she was failing as a mother. Glancing over at the crib, she struggled to hold back her tears. Her precious daughter, Olha, was warmly snuggled down under the blanket, sleeping gently and innocently, unaware of the problems being caused.

Knowing how anxious his wife was becoming about the issues of the baby's night-time crying, Myroslaw spoke to a couple of his Ukrainian friends on their weekend meet up. A good friend of the couple suggested they could stay with him and his family. They had quite a large house and several of the Ukrainians newcomers had also been staying with them.

As a quick fix to the problem and the darkened atmosphere that had arisen at their lodgings, the pair packed up once again and moved the three of them into another new home on Shaw Heath. Maria was relieved for the escape route and a fresh opportunity, and believed living in a household with other Ukrainians would be a pleasant change.

Thankfully, baby Olha soon settled in and an end to the disturbed nights finally came. The move had fixed many issues, they both thought, each of them gaining a good night's sleep.

The women in the house got on tremendously well together. They all shared the task of cooking for the household, making some delicious Ukrainian dishes to divide between them. Once all the children were fed, bathed, and settled, they would happily spend their evenings together. The women singing their hearts out or sitting together chattering whilst carefully completing embroidery cloths.

Maria sat deep within the group, totally involved and accepted. As she threaded the fine wool through her embroidery needle, she thought back to the evenings she had spent as a child, sat warm and cosy beside the fire, intrigued, watching her Mama. She would weave tiny stitches of woollen threads through a piece of cloth that lay upon her lap, slowly becoming a useful item of beautiful colour. Those evenings had taught her well.

Using coloured threads, specific for their individual regional homeland localities. The women's activity involved needle weaving stitches, following symbolic patterns of geometric motifs, zigzags, crosses, and floral patterns. Embroideries rich history had been a huge part of their families for generations. It was used for preserving national identity in folk clothing, blouses and aprons and beautifying their homes as a decorative element, making pillowcases, tablecloths and towels and shrouds for icons in churches.

The men, with their serious expressions, gathered deep in conversation. Life seemed to be moving along merrily. Each of them enjoying the kind support and the company of their new housemates.

However, within a few months Maria sadly noticed a change. They were spending more and more time within the household and less time together as a couple. Whilst it had initially been a very welcomed change, it couldn't go on forever if they were to make their marriage work. Maria had also noticed Myroslaws nightmares were regularly returning.

Spending so much time in the company of his fellow Ukrainians, he had begun to enjoy a tipple of whiskey, all too often. Maria felt the alcohol was opening the lid on his memories, his anger and hurt at losing his homeland.

Stirring up wounds that still hadn't healed or been properly discussed.

Maria felt desperate to have a home and a space of their own and couldn't help but feel disappointed that their money was being wasted on this needless drink when it could have been saved towards a house deposit. This annoyance to Maria became too much. She could no longer hide it.

Early one Sunday morning, the pair were out for an early morning walk, heading down towards the local park. Myroslaw strolled beside Maria, his arms stretched as he pushed along the pram. Olha sat quietly, taking in the surroundings.

As they reached the bench just inside the park, Maria suggested they take a seat. Myroslaw knew something was about to be discussed. Maria hadn't been her usual happy self lately.

She didn't want to be cross with Myroslaw, he was everything she wanted in a husband. Sitting up tight by his side, she turned to face him, brushing a stray lock from his forehead for closeness. "I'm not upset with you Slawko, but I'm tired of this situation, I know the last few months have been especially hard for you, but we can't carry on like this, drinking is not the answer, and I won't allow it to interfere with our marriage," she stated, quite matter of fact in their own language.

Myroslaw agreed, partially to keep Maria happy, but he knew she was right. The drinking needed to stop. He enjoyed the support and encouragement he'd received from the new housemates, but the lodgings had only ever been a temporary measure. He agreed, they did need to save and work towards having a home of their own. As much as they both loved the company they had in the lodging, it didn't do them any good as a family. They had to move on.

Within six months of moving in, the couple were once again packing up and moving out.

Mr and Mrs Maksimovich were also fellow Ukrainians living at Shaw Heath. They were more than happy to rent out a room to them.

Mrs Maksimovich had given birth to a son, Bohdan, in the same month that Olha had been born. Without her income also coming into their house, it had been a stretch to pay the mortgage, so this additional rental payment would be a huge bonus to the household.

Even though the women got along very well, Maria could see a sadness in Mrs Maksimovich, she hadn't been feeling well for some time, however with a small baby to take care of she couldn't afford to take time out to care for herself more. Maria knew only too well how tiring being a mother could be, but Bohdan was generally an easy baby and she thought it may be more than just tiredness. Maria didn't want to meddle in the couple's affairs, it wasn't her business to get involved in.

Thankfully, she didn't need to.

A few weeks later, Mr Maksimovich accompanied his wife to her doctor's appointment late one afternoon. The doctor immediately referred her to St Thomas hospital for a short stay to support her through her baby blues.

Whilst she was away, Maria did her best to help around the house and cooking the meals. Mr Maksimovich had taken several days off work in recent weeks. His employers, with their lack of support and understanding, were becoming frustrated by his regular absence. Maria had offered help with baby Bohdan whenever she could.

Olha was almost a year old, and Maria thought it was as good a time as any to return to employment.

She had asked around locally for work and found a position available at Welkin Mill. Ideally, the mill also had a nursery for the children to stay in during the workday and at one-year-old, they would take Olha. As an employee at the Mill, the charge was discounted. And a small fee would be deducted directly from Maria's salary.

With his wife needing more hospital care, Mr Maksimovich was becoming more reliant on Maria for her help. Upon hearing the news of Maria's new employment, he asked Maria if she would take Bohdan to the nursery with Olha. Maria was only too happy to help the family out, with Mr Maksimovich paying the full amount for Bohdan to join Olha in the nursery.

A couple of weeks later, and with a new routine set, the days back at a mill began.

A small green bus would arrive at the end of the cobbled back street. By 6am each morning Maria would be carefully fastening the one-year-olds into the seats, safely and securely, ready for the journey to Lower Bredbury, to the nursery where they would be spending their daytimes. She was thankful for the morning bus service included in the fees; it meant she could have a little spare time alone.

She would hastily run back into the lodgings to peel and prepare the vegetables for the evening meal. She would tidy around the kitchen, wash through and hang out nappies, anything she could find time to do whilst she was alone in the house for an hour.

By 7am her shoes were fastened and Maria was rushing over to the mill to begin her shift, usually meeting her work mates along the way. Idle chatter filled the walk. It felt good to have adult company once again.

At lunch time Maria would nip across to the nursery, a large old building adjoining the mill. She would peep inside through the large windows to check that Olha and Bohdan were happy. Usually catching them both sitting side by side, eating their lunch before being settled down on a mattress for their afternoon nap. Comforted by seeing the children settled and taken care of, she would return to the mill.

Early evening after finishing her shift, Maria would rush over to collect the children, often getting remarks about *the twins*, many people mistaking the two youngsters for siblings.

The pair played happily together back home and once Mr Maksimovich had returned home from work, he would take Bohdan for his wash and share a bedtime read with his son. Giving Maria some precious time to spend with Olha, singing her sweet lullabies before putting her snuggly into her crib for the evening.

Mr Maksimovich contributed greatly to the grocery shop for the household in return, thankful to Maria for her generous help. He made sure there was always plenty of food in the pantry. It helped a lot financially and allowed Maria and Myroslaw the opportunity to begin saving a little for a deposit, for a home of their own.

4
Buying A First Home

1953

Holding onto a set of keys had never felt so exciting. They had done it. They'd both worked many hours and saved hard. With the addition of the extra amount needed being kindly gifted to them from Auntie Elsie's generous parents, they had managed to get a deposit together themselves and pay in full for their new home. Securing a home of their very own at the total price of £50.

This had been their dream for some time, a house of their own, a place where they could grow their family.

Myroslaw had learned a small amount of English by now, mainly at work. He had gained confidence in the language that Maria was yet to master. Having had time away from work to care for the baby and any spare time spent with Ukrainian friends, she didn't need to use the language. It wasn't something she wanted to learn or particularly use; she was happy to stay with her own language for now and without the tutoring from her previous landlady Elsie she had seemingly lost the urge to learn.

It was an icy cold January morning. Wrapped up warm, the pair and their toddler left the solicitor's office in

Edgeley and headed across town, in the direction of Hillgate.

Olha, at a little over two and a half, was used to walking, but her little legs soon tired on the journey, so Myroslaw carried her the rest of the way.

Arriving at 15 Bamford Street, Myroslaw handed the keys over to Maria, her face gleaming with happiness.

It was a small, terraced house, each house on the street looked identical. Neither of them had seen terraced houses before they had arrived in Britain. It had seemed the strangest thing to have neighbours close by, let alone adjoining houses and with no gardens or fields around them, it felt quite bleak.

Their excitement was short-lived as they eagerly turned the key and opened the front door.

They had been for a look at the house from the outside a few weeks prior, only having the chance to try and look through the filthy windows.

There was a long waiting list to view the property. At such a reasonable price, they had jumped at the opportunity. Taking a gamble, they placed an offer before an official viewing. The offer had been immediately accepted. This was the first time they had stepped foot inside. The terrible smell of damp and mould immediately hit them, clutching at their throats.

Maria stepped over to the darkened window and opened the threadbare curtains further, to try and let in some light. Then instructed Myroslaw not to put Olha down from his arms, not allowing her daughter to experience such dirty conditions.

The carpets, thick with grime and dirt, obviously hadn't felt a broom brushed along them for many years. The limp wallpaper looked to be hanging off the walls, black mould lining the tops of the paper below the ceiling.

They walked into the back room of the house, into the small kitchen area. The walls were painted eggshell, with huge cracks running across in several directions that made it apparent no one had thought about this room for some time.

The kitchen held a small stove; Maria wasn't sure that, even with her efforts cleaning it, it would ever be usable. To the side of the stove was a tall pantry cupboard, shelves caked in grungy, sticky coverings.

There was a small window and door to the back wall. Maria unlocked the door, imagining a small area at least that Olha could play safely in during the summer months.

Disappointed, the couple stepped out into the shared courtyard. Stepping along the stone paved area slightly, they came to the neighbour's door and a small outbuilding housing the outside toilet for the two houses to share.

Neither of them spent too long looking inside. They had seen enough and would deal with the dreaded toilet as and when they needed to do so.

Back inside the house, Myroslaw took the lead upstairs, using the staircase to the side of the kitchen. The top of the house at least had two separate bedroom spaces, although only the front bedroom had a doorway and door. The second bedroom opened directly onto the landing area, with just a banister rail, it had no wall, no doorway. At least it was a separate area, however, a curtain across would surely give them some privacy in the future. Both rooms were small and drab, with the carpets and wallpaper in a similar poor condition like downstairs.

There was certainly going to be a lot of work ahead for it to reach a liveable condition, but hard work was something the couple weren't afraid of.

Having seen all that, they needed to see for today; they hastily closed the front door behind them. Both taking a mental note of the hard work ahead of them. This was their home, and it would soon be the smartest, cleanest, most welcoming house on the street. They were both certain of that.

Having been innocently unaware of the huge amount of work that was facing them, they had already informed Mr

Maksimovich of their departure. With his wife currently back at home and in better health to care for Bohdan, it was ideal timing, and they already had new tenants ready and able and moving in on their departure at the end of the week. They now realised they had been unrealistic in thinking they would be able to move in so soon. A temporary home needed to be found quickly.

Thankfully, Myroslaw soon found them a short-term lodging on Tame Street, Portwood, with some other Ukrainian friends, whilst they cleaned up the house and at least made it bearable, if not liveable.

Maria had left her job at the mill recently, finding the care of two small children, running a home for two families and working full time just too much. Wanting to spend more time with her precious daughter and more time making their new house a home, they had agreed that she would take some time off.

The saving had been done, and they were used to budgeting so they were sure they would survive just fine on the one wage for a while.

***

Over the following few weeks, Maria and Olha's days were spent at the new house as Maria began her cleaning mission. After trying without success to open the windows, years of caked on paint had made it impossible to budge. She had to scrape away at the paint, just to allow some air into the rooms. The carpets being so full of fleas and mites proved to be impossible to clear and clean of such nuisances and so needed to be removed and the floorboards cleaned thoroughly with disinfectant.

Maria was keen to be living in their own home as soon as they possibly could. She would spend long days scrubbing and mopping whilst Olha played happily or sat watching her Mama work.

The stove alone took her a whole day to clean, years of grease and grim completely smothered it. The oven with just one shelf was black with a thick char. Maria was pleased with herself by the end of the day, that at least if they could get the stove working, it was now clean enough to cook meals safely.

On one busy Saturday morning, having decided to remove the grubby, mouldy wallpaper, Maria laid a small blanket on the freshly disinfected floor and settled Olha to play with the doll that Auntie Elsie had thoughtfully bought the little girl. She began to peel off the damp wall covering. The paper came off very easily, revealing behind it, the most disgusting home of crawling insects, cockroaches, woodlice, and fleas. All hopping around and trying to escape the safety they had found under the paper.

In a panic, Maria came up with a plan; she would set fire to the remaining paper coverings drifting from the walls, to kill off the infestations.

Soon realising her mistake, Maria struggled to put out the fire. Smoke began bellowing, filling the room, the angry flames dancing about. Rushing, she quickly took Olha out into the back and returned with a mop bucket full of water. Thankfully, after several panicked bucket loads the fire was safely extinguished and having removed the carpets days earlier, the fire soon fizzled out.

Maria rushed to open the doors and windows to allow the smoke to seep out into the street. Standing shaking outside with Olha safely in her arms, she cried with fear. She could have seriously harmed or killed them both, she realised.

Myroslaw, finished his shift later that afternoon and arrived at the house. He was greeted by the strong smell of smoke. Relief washed over him to see his wife and daughter were both unharmed. However, the smoke had at least cleared some of the vermin for now. The couple would need to find another method to remove the rest of them.

The house currently wasn't a great place for a small toddler to be. There was so much work to be done and they had to do it all as soon as they could. Previously, Maria had on a couple of occasions asked Rosa to look after Olha whilst she ran an errand or suchlike, trusting her wholeheartedly, but Rosa had recently met a nice young gentleman and was spending her limited free time courting. Maria was truly happy for her friend and so didn't want to disturb the growing romance.

But the couple decided they needed help with childcare whilst the work was completed.

Myroslaw suggested they request a few hours of help from Auntie Elsie at the weekend. She was more than happy to help the couple out and cherished the thought of spending time with this beautiful little girl that she had become so fond of. They were most grateful for her support.

They had all become good friends recently. Auntie Elsie had previously invited them to share her family's evening meal, at the large semi-detached house she shared with her elderly parents. The night had been huge success and as they all had an enjoyable time, it had become a weekly event which they all looked forward to. Having no grandchildren of their own to spoil, the elders especially, counted the days until they next saw their guests. They thoroughly enjoyed watching Olha play with the dolls that they had kindly bought for her.

The family returned to the sitting room after a delicious meal. The couple relaxing by the fire and Olha playing on the thick woollen rug in the middle of the room. They both wished they had a home a cosy and welcoming as this.

Work began the following weekend. The house was soon cleared of any living creatures and mites or as many as were possible. The walls were stripped and freshly painted in a clean white emulsion, large woollen rugs were laid in the front room and bedrooms, to give a warm cosy feel. Searching in the second-hand shops, the couple soon gathered a couple of beds, a sofa and wooden chair for the front room.

Their home sweet home was finally ready for the young family and within a month of picking up the keys, they were happily closing their very own front door to the world and at last having time to themselves.

The following day, however, late on a Sunday afternoon, there was a loud rapping on the front door.

With Maria busy in the kitchen preparing the grated beetroot to make a pan of Borscht for the evening meal.

Myroslaw, who was arranging a fire in the grate, stood to open the door. Standing on the pavement outside was a familiar face, Constable Jones. He had been a regular visitor to each of their lodgings many times and having been informed of their new address, officially needed to visit and complete an update report.

"Come in, please," requested Myroslaw politely.

As usual, he quickly invited the police officer into his home and out of sight of the new neighbours, knowing that there would possibly be questions and gossips to come in the next few days. On hearing the voices, Maria had put the water pot onto the stove to heat, in readiness to offer a cup of tea to their visitor.

Constable Jones, although calling on official business had become quite close to the couple over the last five years. It was upon his recommended clearance that Myroslaw had been given the opportunity to thrive, having proved himself to be a useful and decent member of the Stockport community. He saw no harm in the husband and father he witnessed, being committed to providing the best life he could for his little family.

Two cups of strong, milky tea later, with the relevant paperwork completed and identity cards stamped, Constable Jones picked up the peaked hat that he had laid on the seat beside him. Placing it back on his head, the gleaming crown badge to the front of the peak grabbed the light in the room as he straightened it.

He bid the couple a good evening, reminding them he would be back to see them again in a week or two.

With the door once again closed to the street, Maria hurried back into the kitchen to finish off the soup, with the beetroot and meat simmering away nicely, Maria asked Myroslaw to carry the tin bath into the front room for Olha's bath time. He placed it in front of the warm fire.

Maria & Myroslaws Identity Cards for National Registration

Maria & Olha on the steps of Bamford Street

Maria had been filling a bucket with boiled hot water whilst the visitor had been chatting to Myroslaw. With no running hot water in the house, bath time took a long time to prepare.

She bathed Olha in the warm, shallow water and, sitting by the fireside, attentively dried off and dressed the toddler in fresh nightwear. Taking her daughter with her back into the kitchen whilst she finished off the meal, she closed the door to the front room, so Myroslaw could use the now tepid bath water himself, with some privacy. Maria would use the water the next bath time, with the unexpected visitor arriving, the evening meal was already late enough for Olha's bedtime.

By Summer the family had settled into the house well. They thoroughly enjoyed their own space and had made good friends with the neighbours along the street. A new addition had also been added to the household, a small black cat, not a pet as such, more a guard to keep away the rats from the back courtyard.

The couple were happy and content with their lives.

The neighbourhood began arranging a party at Chapel Hall, just across the street from their house. Maria loved an excuse for a party and gladly volunteered to help with the food preparations.

As the morning of the Queen's Coronation arrived, all having eaten breakfast, she left Olha sat in the kitchen with Myroslaw.

Carefully, carrying her food items, she joined the other housewives who were busily making sandwiches over at the Hall. Maria had offered to donate a couple of loaves of bread and a pot of jam for the gathering. Thinking nothing of the fact that they could little afford to be giving away these items, the family had been eagerly awaiting this special royal day. Today was a day of excitement and these types of days didn't come along that often. She was looking forward to them all spending the afternoon with their good neighbours, a chance to relax and have some fun.

Back at the house, Olha, who had recently turned three, sat by the wooden table in the kitchen. She didn't often have time with just her Tato, and she watched, mesmerised as Myroslaw shaved his dark, stubbly cheeks and chin over the kitchen sink. A few minutes later, with a hand towel, he dabbed the remaining froth from his face, checking in the small mirror leaning on the kitchen windowsill. This was a daily routine for Myroslaw, but today he wanted to make sure he looked his very best. There hadn't been a special occasion to celebrate for some time.

He wasn't a huge fan of socialising at parties and felt a little nervous. He had got to know a few of the neighbours, and they all seemed to have been most welcoming to them. Even though his understanding of the English language had grown, he still struggled to follow conversations, let alone join in with it. He didn't want anyone to think him stupid. Today was going to be a tough day. He knew if he told Maria how he was feeling, she would just tell him to relax and enjoy it. She was so lively and confident; her lack of this new language mainly didn't faze her, and she just thrived by being surrounded by people.

Whether they understood each other or not, there was always some sort of understanding. Just after eleven o'clock Maria arrived back from her sandwich making duties. She beamed with excitement and playfully scooped up Olha, who still quietly sat by the table and now watching her Tato polishing his shiny black shoes.

Picking up Olha and twirling her around in her arms, Maria began singing, songs she often sang to her little girl, songs that made her feel good, both of them sharing the happiest of smiles.

With less than an hour until the party began, there was little time to waste. Leaving Myroslaw to his shoe polishing, she made her way upstairs with her daughter in her arms, grabbing the wet face cloth from the draining board on her way. Laying neatly upon the beds were their clothes. None were party clothes, none were new, but they were all clean and fresh, which was all that mattered to Maria.

A short time later, cleaned and dressed for the occasion, a smart-looking mother and daughter made their way back down the steep stairs. Olha's shoulder length hair draping yellow ribbons through her carefully plaited hair.

Myroslaw gave a teasing whistle to the pair as they entered the kitchen, looking lovely.

Maria beamed. Pleased by her husband's playful response, she gave him a quick kiss on the cheek, telling him to go and get ready himself or they would be late.

Today is going to be a wonderful day, she thought to herself.

5
Missing The Motherland

Life had never been easy in Ukraine, but in Maria's heart it was the place she had always lovingly called 'Home.' Her heart ached for the beauty of Ukraine.

A Ukrainian can't live without nature. Can't live without or detach from the green meadows, the gently flowing streams, the beautiful fragrance of wildflowers and harvesting crops.

The sound of birds singing sweetly in a quiet and peaceful village. A place where dreams waited, hopeful for the chance to blossom.

A far distance away in miles, but always so close by in Maria's thoughts and memories. Despite the cruel and difficult start to her life, she painted a perfect childhood with simple pleasures, close family, neighbours and hospitality.

Maria had been born to parents Johanna and Matvij in March 1926. Her birth had taken place in the family home, in a small, idyllic village, in Nyrkiv, Western Ukraine. Peacefully nestled amidst the colourful meadows and the tranquil embrace of its nature.

Time danced to the rhythm of traditions and harmony of a close-knit Greek Catholic community.

Beautiful melodies spread through the air of the village, carrying many tales of joy and sorrow.

The family home was a humble and inviting wooden house at the end of a dirt paved lane. To the back of the house lay vast fields, crops carefully tendered to by the small, young family. At the far end of the fields, a stream flowed gently by; perfect for washing clothes and bathing on a warm day.

Life was basic in this agrarian neighbourhood. A stone well in front of the home provided them with endless fresh water. Chickens roamed loosely in the front yard, on the lookout for grain to peck. To the side of the house, a large wooden outbuilding stored a heavy, old, rusted plough, a well-stacked wood store and a large timber box to store the grain.

Family home in Ukraine

Family Funeral Procession, escorting the deceased to the cemetery in the village

Inside the house, the main room had a large clay fire stove, perfectly set up for cooking the family's meals and providing warmth throughout the home. An extension to the stove provided an additional planked sleeping area, the warmest of beds in the house. A small but cosy room where the family would spend most of their time together in the evenings, after a long day working the fields. Beyond the living area were two bedroom areas, a long embroidered sheet hung across the doorway, to give a small amount of privacy

The closest neighbours lived just a short stroll down along the lane, sharing this beautiful, idyllic hamlet. Each resident holding the same values and deep-rooted beliefs.

Several previous generations of both Johanna and Matvijs families had lived in Nyrkiv and the neighbouring village of Nahoryany for centuries.

Johanna's parents, Kurilo Analiy and Marianna, had passed away in recent years. Leaving behind Johanna and her three elder brothers. Both Kurilo and Marianna had been from large families, with dozens of family members scattered between the two villages. Each of the offspring worked hard on their land to provide for their large households, tied to farming and connecting to nature.

Matviy's parents, Theodorius Lavuta and Maria, had also passed away recently. Leaving behind their grown-up children and their families. Ivan, Matvijs brother, was married to Agifia, and they lived in Nahoryany with their nine small children. His sister Anna was also married with several children. She lived close by in Nyrkiv. life was difficult.

It had been a wonderful surprise for the young parents when Johanna discovered she was pregnant again. Matvij and Johanna were thrilled when Maria Kateryna had been born safely, a beautiful, much yearned for, healthy baby daughter.

After many years of trying unsuccessfully for another baby, their prayers had finally been answered. A miracle sibling for Yaroslaw, an older brother by eight years.

Johanna adored being a mother and cherished spending as much time as she could with her new-born baby.

Spare time was sparse. So much work needed completing to keep her children and husband fed, but young Yaroslaw had been a great help to his father.

He would happily join his Tato working, spending long, tiring hours on the land, often returning to the house after dark.

This allowed Johanna at least some precious time to bond with her new bundle and time to prepare the family a good meal for the end of the working day.

Finishing the morning chores by lunch time, Johanna would snuggle the baby down into a sheet sling. Wrapped closely around her own body, holding her little one warm and close, she would carefully take her along into the fields to join Yaroslaw, and Matvij. Carrying with her some bread, meat and a jug filled with fresh, cool water from the well.

The warm sun cast a soft, golden glow over the colourful flowering meadows. Spring had certainly arrived.

The family would gather closely and sit down on the soft, plush grass together for a welcome lunchtime break. Soaking up the rays of the sunshine and relaxing in the beauty of nature.

Once they had all eaten and rested a little, she would help them to plant crops or gather the ripe vegetables, with baby Maria sleeping peacefully by her side.

Johanna had a huge amount of love for the little family they had created, often scooping up Yaroslaw for a hug, much to his disproval, at eight years old he saw himself as a worker like his father and didn't want to be babied by his mother.

Matvij would laughingly tease him, "Mama's boy," whilst loving the amount of care that his wife managed to spread between them all.

The first few years of Maria's life had been carefree, her parents were very happily married. It was Johanna's sole responsibility to care for the children, keep the house in clean order, and cook the family meals. She was fantastic at planning and organising and would spend several weeks after the harvest, stewing and pickling the fresh fruits and vegetables that had been collected. Placing them into glass jars, ready to be stored and eaten during the long winter months to come.

Johanna had been taught to cook by her own mother, watching and helping her as a young girl, had given her the valuable gift for making some good, tasty, Ukrainian dishes and had taught her a lesson that no food ever went to waste.

Matvij was a tall, dark-haired, well well-built man, whose real strength was proven in the heavy, manual machinery he used each day on the land. Inside of his home was a different story. He was a kind and gentle family man. He had a huge love for his wife and was proud of the strong, loyal woman and mother she was.

There wasn't a huge variety on the menu. A hot meal of Vareniki, soft potato dumplings, smothered with a layer of sizzling, soft buttery onions or a pan of hot tasty Borscht, a hearty thick soup made with grated beetroot and a ham shank, would be waiting for him on his return from the fields each day. He was never disappointed.

Crossing themselves, the family would say a prayer together before their evening meal, seated below the icon. Decorated with an embroidered Rushnyk towel that hung above the wooden table and benches. Thankful that they were blessed with enough food to fill their stomachs, knowing how fortunate they were.

Matvij loved nothing more than to spend time with his wife and children, sitting together in front of the roaring fire in the evening and happily playing his accordion. He knew the joyful tunes would break the silence in the room of tired faces and bring a huge smile to his wife as well as entertainment for the children who loved to listen and watch Tato playing familiar folk music.

Watching his beautiful wife, absorbing the atmosphere, Johanna relaxed to the uplifting strains of the music. Her long, wavy blonde hair uncovered from her headscarf and let loose, draping down past her shoulders after a day tightly held in plaits.

Johanna loved to sing and would cuddle her children into her arms tightly. As they watched Tato losing himself to the melodies, she would break out into a cheerful song. Songs that she had sung for years, songs that had been sung by her parents and their parents too.

Treasured moments like this were the most valuable of times.

Comfortable in the warmth and security of their home, the tired, yawning, children would soon fall asleep to the gentle, soothing, sweet sounds surrounding them.

The couple would together carry the sleeping children to the bed they shared in the next room. Covering them with woollen blankets and each placing a goodnight kiss on the children's foreheads. Once they were warmly tucked in and the flicker of the bedside candle was blown out, the couple would return to spend some precious time together before sleep called the end of the night.

***

The age gap between the two siblings became more and more obvious, as Maria began toddling around and wanting to play with her big brother.

Yaroslaw was feeling far too grown up for playing childish games, instead he was loving the time he spent working with his father. He loved being outdoors, breathing in the fresh air. When Tato ever suggested for him to stay behind at home to help his Mama, whilst he went to tend the fields, he would grumble. He wanted to be out exploring the village, working on the land and helping, not in the yard being his little sister's playmate.

Life was a constant routine of hard work for the young family, but they were happy and content and shortly after Maria's fifth birthday, the arrival of a new baby completed the family unit.

The couple named the small baby boy Vasyl, Maria instantly fell in love with her perfect little brother. She would fuss over him, more than happy to help Mama wash and take care of him, singing him lullabies to sooth him to sleep after Mama had fed him.

6
Holodomor - Death By Hunger

1932

Life can turn and bite you when you least expect it.

Joseph Stalin had wanted to replace Ukraine's small farms with state run collectives.

Police and communist apparatchiks ransacked the homes of peasants, taking away everything edible, placing them on blacklists and preventing them from receiving any food.

The peasants in these small villages were forbidden to leave to search for food further afield. The soviet officials had informed them that the famine had something to do with the drying crops, the bad farming, the weather, anything to cover their obvious tracks. But the village people had seen and heard of harvests being taken away to regions where the people were felt to be more valuable, more deserving of food or so they were disgustingly told.

The chickens had long since been eaten, it seemed a sensible idea to eat them before they were abruptly taken from them.

With no bread in the house, the only earlier option had been to live on potatoes and potato cakes. Leaving the potatoes hidden in the soil for as long as was possible, so as not to be found and taken away from them.

It became a regular journey to go into the forests foraging for mushrooms and berries, anything edible.

It was a hopeless state to be living in.

Johanna and Matvij tried to hide their constant hunger from the children, so as not to cause them worry and upset, feeding the children before themselves. However, the children soon became anaemic and began complaining of dizziness.

***

As time marched on and desperation set in, Joanna would cook the family a bitter porridge mixture from Goosefoot and Acacia leaves and make soups, consisting of any leaves or weeds they had managed to collect, with the hope that the hunger pains would ease for a short time. The family would also eat at any blossom that they managed to source on their hunt for food.

The village soon became bare of any edible finds, rivers that once flowed carrying fish had been emptied. The wild animals that once roamed within the forests, seemed non-existent, presumably they had already been hunted down and had settled groaning stomachs somewhere nearby.

The flowers, tree bark and grass were an option and a pleasant find to the lucky person.

They soon learned to accept the hunger. There was nothing they could do but to try their hardest and survive. The anger welled up inside, as they let go of their dignity with as much ease as their pride would allow them.

Too weak to make the long, painful journeys, Matvij and Johanna would take it in turns to venture out to neighbouring villages, desperate for any findings. Knowing this venturing was forbidden, they felt the chance was one they had no option but to take. Often, they returned home more horrified than when they set off, discovering many along the way, hadn't been so lucky to survive the genocide.

***

By the spring of 1933, the famine had been exposed to other countries. Stalin finally decided to lower grain delivery targets and began dispatching some relief, although this didn't make its way to the peasants who were in need. The genocide ended as quickly as it had begun.

It was truly a miracle; their prayers had been answered and the family were all thankfully still alive.

Alive in the sense that they all still had breath in their weak, bony bodies, nothing else, but they had survived.

A year of hunger, starving for months and watching the family wasting away with time.

Life began to improve with a flickering hope, crops began to erupt from the redundant soils. Food supplies increased slightly, as did the energy to begin life again where it had been paused.

However, rations and starvation had caused many ailments and illnesses that sadly couldn't be cured in many families.

The man of the house, Matvij, having suffered in silence for some months, so as not to cause concern to his family, sadly passed away.

Maria, losing her father at just seven-years-old was lost and confused in her young thoughts

He left behind his devoted wife, Johanna, to bring up their three children alone. Vasyl, at just two-years-old was too young to know anything about the huge event that had taken place, but Yaroslaw, aged fifteen, was completely devastated.

After such a painful, worrying time the last couple of years, the light at the end of the tunnel had been swiftly dimmed by his death. Each of their hearts, as gloomy as the evening sky that had brought an end to that sad day.

Johanna sent Yaroslaw to call at the village undertaker's house and inform him of the death of his Tato. It was the undertaker's duty to inform the doctor from the neighbouring village and arrange a visit at the deceased house to confirm the death. It was also his task to instruct the local artisans to make a coffin and wooden cross for the grave over the next couple of days. As it was getting late in the evening, informing the local priest would wait until daylight as would the ringing of the church bells.

As the family huddled together tightly, awaiting a visit from the doctor to officiate the death, Johanna stood up and walked towards the fire. Reaching out, she picked up the metal kettle of fresh water, carefully placing it above the flames to boil in readiness for cleansing Matvijs body and prepare him for his burial.

Within the hour, the unusual sound of a motor vehicle engine could be heard arriving outside the house, signalling the approach of a person of importance. With the clunk of the vehicle door, the doctor was there. Yaroslaw greeted him and ushered him inside, carrying a brown doctor's bag.

Johanna showed the doctor through to their bedroom where Matviy lay. She stood to the side to allow him to complete his examination. Minutes later, the doctor moved away from the bed.

"I will record the death in the morning. You will need to collect the certificate from my office tomorrow afternoon," he instructed her rather bluntly, busily packing his examination items into his bag. Obviously wanting to get back to his bed for the night.

Johanna nodded, feeling empty of words in reply.

"May he rest in god," he offered to the family as he quietly left the house.

It was almost midnight. Silence had smothered the house. Little Vasyl had fallen asleep cuddled up by Maria's side, her arms wrapped warmly around him, as much for her own comfort.

Johanna and the older children shared the evenings prayer together, then after kissing each of them, she carried Vasyl to the bed and said a goodnight to Maria and Yaroslaw as they too climbed in to sleep.

Collecting a washing bowl, Johanna poured out the hot water from the metal kettle and placed the bowl on the bedroom dresser. She lit a candle and placed it at the head of the bed. Reaching inside the wooden chest, its lid of flowers as beautiful as the day she had painstakingly painted them, she removed a fresh shirt and trousers for her husband to be dressed in for his burial. She felt completely numb as she bathed and dressed his body, knowing it was a ritual that she had to follow. Looking up towards the icon above the bed, she crossed herself, feeling some comfort and strength to continue.

She placed a linen sheet, covering the body up to the chin, touching his thick dark hair, smoothing it neatly into place. After a final kiss on the cold lips of her husband, Johanna finally draped a white cloth over his face, neck and shoulders.

Carrying the bowl of water outside, Johanna walked over to the far end of the outhouse to emptying the contents into a remote place, where no people or animals would tread the soil.

Back inside, Johanna brought in a rickety wooden stool from the food store and placed it beside the bed. Perching down upon it she rested besides her husband's body, here she would stay for the few remaining hours of the night.

Within a few hours, the church bells were chiming loudly, giving an announcement of the death to the village folk. Johanna stirred from her light sleep. *Word will soon pass throughout the village,* she thought to herself. Neatening her hair and covering it with a black headscarf, she then used the remainder of the water, now cold, from the kettle and dampened a cloth to wipe clean her face.

Today would see a flurry of friends and relatives, each wanting to pay their respects to the deceased.

The children awoke wearily. Walking silently past his Mama, Yaroslaw headed straight out and into the yard. He sat on the bench to the front of the house, a place where his Tato would often sit after his early morning porridge, listening to the birds singing and gathering his energy before his day's work. This morning though, even the birds had gone silent. Yaroslaw didn't know what he felt, but somehow, he felt at ease sitting on this bench at this moment.

Vasyl had woken up hungry, as he did every day. A growing toddler. Maria noted the quiet atmosphere, Mama was slow, quiet, and Maria didn't know what to say. She had so many questions she wanted ask, but she didn't know quite how to voice them.

Instead, she grabbed hold of the large metal pot and began cooking the porridge. Believing her Mama would appreciate the help at this time and hopefully settling her hungry little brother. His young years were oblivious to the goings on around him.

With the door to the house left open, the day of respectful mourning visitors soon began.

Relatives came and went throughout the day. Friends of Matvij and the family had heard the sad news and presented themselves to view the body. Each crossing themselves as they recalled the Lord's prayer before entering the house.

As the evening dusk drew in, the extended family gathered in and around the house by the front yard. A member of the family stayed, always present and sitting beside the deceased. A custom that had been followed for generations. A deceased body should never be left alone in the dark, candles were placed around the room and visitors through the night. At midnight, dinner took place, followed by a vigil for the remainder of the night, until more mourners came to pay their respects in the mourning.

Each of them had brought food parcels along with them.

Once the children had eaten their supper, they washed and got into bed for the night. It had been a busy day of comings and goings. The children, as well as Johanna had received a great many hugs and blessings from the visitors, each in an attempt to sooth their grief somewhat.

The family members stayed through the night and as the sun began to rise, the sound of horse's hooves could be heard clattering as the wheels of the cart thrummed along the lane. The local artisans had arrived with the newly made pine coffin and a carved wooden cross to mark the grave.

The funeral procession began just before noon at the family home. The priest's words accompanied a scattering of incense and sprinkles of holy water, as the body was lifted into the coffin.

Relatives circled the coffin, each holding lit candles before them, as they said prayers for Matviy's journey to god's garden.

Following the large wooden cross, the family trailed behind the coffin, carried on the strong shoulders of the pall bearers.

The procession stopped briefly, part way along the journey, taking time in front of the village church for the priest to recite a prayer of departure.

Arriving at the cemetery with the freshly dug grave, the priest blessed the grave, and the coffin was lowered to the ground. Each of the relatives took a handful of earth and as it was thrown onto the coffin, the mourners joined in with the hymn Vichnaya Pamyat—eternal memory.

The neighbours showed a great deal of kindness to the family, but after receiving a lifetime of hugs and kind blessings from them all, Johanna just wanted to spend some time alone with her children. Time for them to grieve together in private.

Yaroslaw walked on ahead in a daze, whilst Johanna and the children strolled hand in hand for the short walk back from the cemetery. Back home, Johanna closed the door behind them. The last twenty-four hours had been truly unbelievable, each of them was in shock at the truth of this reality.

After a fitful night's sleep in Matvijs fireside chair, the dawn light broke through the small gap in the curtains. Johanna went into the back room to check on the children. Each of them was still sound asleep. The previous day's emotions had obviously taken its toll on them.

Leaving them in their innocent and peaceful state, she heated some water on the fire and began making some porridge for when they awoke.

Glancing at Matvijs muddy old work boots to the side of the back door, sadness smothered her, realising he wouldn't be stepping into them this morning, or any morning ever again. She battled with herself to stop the tears filling her eyes.

There was to be no time for grieving, no lying in bed all day with falling tears, life couldn't sit still.

From now on, life was increasingly difficult for Johanna, without her husband's strong hands working on the land and her suffering persistent pains in her stomach; some days she felt almost paralysed with the pain, unsure what was causing this worrying agony.

However, she had no other option but to drag her frail, weary body to the fields, delegating some of the smaller chores to the young children to help her a little. The ever-cheerful toddler Vasyl kept the front yard neatly swept. Maria was more than happy to give help to her Mama, collecting the freshly grown vegetables and delicious ripe fruits. Digging at the soils the best she could for potatoes.

Yaroslaw, having reached his teens, spent all his time in the fields, taking the death of his Tato, 'his hero', hard, he gladly took his upset and anger out using the heavy machinery, wanting to prove to his Mama he was more than capable of doing the heavy work and taking on the position of the man of the house.

Johanna's stomach pain, gradually worsened, without the option for visiting a doctor, neither having the spare money or a doctor available locally. However, with a young, hungry family to feed, she had little option but to continue with the work in the fields and around the house the best she could. If the crops weren't tended to, they would all go hungry. The children had been an incredible help, making it all a bit more bearable.

It had been a long, tiring day in the fields. Johanna had been keen to collect as many of the harvested fruits as they could before they turned or were eaten by animals. Making sure that they would be able to fill enough jars to put in store for winter. She would begin the pickling and stewing in the morning. Maria and Vasyl, with the endless energy of children, ran up ahead towards the house, leaving an exhausted Mama strolling behind with the harvest baskets in hand.

Each day, a day of routine and chores, the family were coming together to survive until some years later…

7
Easter

<u>1939</u>

The preparations had begun for the Easter celebrations. Johanna and the children were looking forward to the occasion.

The first three days of the week had been very busy. Taking a clean, damp cloth, Johanna had thoroughly wiped clean the wicker basket, in preparation for the delicious food to be laid in it, ready for the blessing at the village Greek Catholic church Easter service. Time had been taken to gently wash a white linen napkin to be placed at the base of the basket for the food to sit upon.

The basket sat perched on the large old wooden sideboard in the food store at the back of the house. The *rushnyk*, a traditional towel that had been affectionately embroidered with Johanna's gentle hands, lay neatly beside the basket in readiness to cover the feast.

Having a mental list in her head, she ticked off the chores that were completed, keeping a note of those that were yet to be done. She had prepared the meat joint she'd been gifted from a family member and it sat spitting as it roasted on a large tin tray, hovering on the fire grate. It filled the house with the most amazingly warm, tasty smell.

The new chickens Johanna had recently acquired at the market in exchange for a few of Tato's old work tools had thankfully produced several freshly laid eggs the previous day.

The eggs had been boiled and were ready for the children to colourfully dye that evening before they headed to bed. Carefully, she wrapped the blocks of butter and cheese into a thin wax paper and placed them into the basket, along with a large horse radish and a small pot of salt. There was no pepper in the house, so this would need to be borrowed from a neighbour. She would send one of the children along to their house later.

Maria was playing outside in the front yard with Vasyl, keeping him occupied as Mama arranged the Easter feast. The pair laughed as they chased the clucking chickens around the yard. Maria wanted to be out in the village playing with their friends, but Mama had told them to stay close by today in case she needed any errands ran.

Yaroslaw had recently met a woman named Anna, a few years older than himself. She was staying in the village with relatives after her grandfather Saveliy had brought her from Chernivtsi, before he headed off to fight for their country.

Yaroslaw and Anna were married shortly thereafter, and they moved into a nearby family house, so Johanna, more than ever, relied on the younger children for help around the house and on the land.

Vasyl had never been to school. Maria had only attended a few times, relishing the raw corn on the cob snack she had been given at break-time, but even she hadn't been for a long time. With no shoes to wear over the winter days, walking to school wasn't a choice they had. Of course, the children were more useful to Johanna at home than at school. Being educated on life skills and running a home was important. School lessons were seen as a privilege and they both, therefore, lacked any formal education.

"Maria," Johanna called out from the house.

On hearing her Mama, Maria skipped over to the house, reaching the open front door.

"Tak, yes Mama," she replied.

"Would you run down to the meadow, please, and find a small willow branch for the basket?"

"Tak! Of course I will, Mama."

Maria, as always, was keen to be a help to Mama and as she raced off in the direction of the field, Vasyl followed closely behind her, always wanting to be in the shadow of the big sister he adored.

Johanna placed a sturdy, white candle down on the sideboard next to the basket. She'd put this in place once the meat and fresh bread cooled and were ready to go in.

Johanna was looking forward to Easter. It had always been her favourite day to celebrate. A time that she would pray for a good harvest ahead. A special occasion that she would spend with other family members. An opportunity for them all to gather and enjoy time with the other village folk, whilst the children could play along the lane and have fun with the others from the village.

The following day, the first day of the Easter festival, Thursday was a very early start as Johanna woke the children. It was 'clean Thursday,' the house needed to be cleaned thoroughly, and so did the youngsters.

Weary eyed, the children jumped out of bed.

"Come, come, Mama needs to get you washed," requested Johanna, turning to leave the room.

Grumbling a little at being so hastily woken, the children followed Mama as she began the stroll towards the stream at the far end of the pasture, breathing in the morning air.

The pleasant morning sun began rising brightly ahead. As they reached the stream, Mama took the cloth and with a dip in the cold water, she began scrubbing each of their faces. The chilly water was quite refreshing, and they were all soon wide awake after the early morning cleanse.

They returned to the house for a warm porridge breakfast before the cleaning day began.

Good Friday was their mourning day. The children with a little rumbling of hunger managed to fast all day. With no work allowed, at least they could reserve some energy. The family spent the day together at church, attending the services being held and meeting with neighbours afterwards. The Mamas gathered, gossiping while the children spent some time playing along the lane.

The family slept through the sunrise the next morning. It was a day of rest so there was no need to be up early, although Johanna was to prepare and bake the traditional Easter bread 'Paska' later that evening and would need to stay awake throughout the night while it baked.

Later that night, once the children were snuggled down warmly in bed for the evening, a worn out Johanna sat down on Tato's chair beside the fire stove, appreciating the warmth that filled the room.

As was a customary tradition, she would be staying awake throughout the night, as her Mother Marianna and Grandmother Kateryna had done in years before her.

A heavenly aroma lingered in the glow of the room as she sat watching the soft dough rising, towering high from the tall cylindrical tin can as it baked.

Exhausted by the efforts of the last few days, Johanna soon reluctantly closed her eyes, checking the mental list in her head.

Had every chore been covered? Had every ritual been followed carefully?
She began dreamily thinking about the exciting days ahead of them all, delicately drifting, falling into a deep sleep, propped up on the old wooden fireside chair, a carefully hand-woven blanket wrapped around her shoulders.

As she snoozed, a crackle from the open fire spat out a glowing ember onto the woven fireside rug, catching fire within a matter of minutes.

The flames soon began racing around the dry, wooden furnished room.

Johanna was totally unaware of the danger and the concerns that lay ahead as she continued dreaming. The flickering fire grabbed onto the draped curtain that had been shutting out the dark of the night, travelling up at speed and scorching at the oak ceiling beam above. As the thick smoke began to fill the room, Johanna's coughing eventually woke her from her sleep.

In a startled state, her first thought was to get the children out of the house and to safety, screaming in a frenzy to wake the children from their beds.

"Vahon, vahon, Fire! get up! get out to the yard," she yelled.

She froze in a panic, standing in the doorway of the room, making sure the children had safely made their way outside. As she tried to register what was happening around her, she turned to leave the room.

Water, she thought. She needed to get water from the well. She hesitated for a moment, trying to gather her thoughts. Her legs trembled below her, making her slim body feel heavy, feeling motionless. Behind her, the fire moved far quicker than the stillness of Johanna's actions. Snapping away at the wood on the ceiling, it caused an old beam to fall away from the corner strut of the front room and hit Johanna. She fell to the ground in a daze, a river of blood gushing from a wound on her head.

She managed to crawl out of the room to the back of the house, moving away from the heat of the fire, dragging herself along the floor to where two frightened children, stood sobbing in the doorway. The fire soon became out of control. Neither knew what to do except to escape the smoke and flames and get to safety. Noting the blood seeping from Mama's head Maria took hold of her shaking hand, Vasyl reached out for her other hand and they both helped her around the back of the house, through the yard and onto the front lane, safely away from the raging fire. Maria left her Mama and Vasyl behind sitting to the side of the lane whilst she sprinted bare foot, to get help from Yaroslaw at his new home.

Within a few minutes, she was hammering uncontrollably on the front door of the small cottage, where her older brother and his wife lived. Unwilling to wait more than a second for someone to come to the door, Maria began screaming.

"Help! help us! Yaroslaw."

Anna was just on her way to bed too, after a sleepless night of baking her Easter bread, Yaroslaw immediately awoke from his deep sleep, recognising his sister's voice, sounding shaky and panicked.

He rushed to the door.

"There's a fire, Mamas hurt," she spluttered. "You need to help us."

Struggling to pull his boots onto his bare feet, Yaroslaw rushed past Maria. Without waiting for any further details, he headed at speed towards the family home.

Reaching the lane, he saw the heavy grey clouds blustering out into the night air, searching up ahead for his Mama and Vasyl, his eyes straining towards the plumes of smoke.

Relief was found at the sight of Mama and his young brother sat huddled in each other's arms on the dirt path, their wide eyes glazed with tears and fright.

Maria, having chased behind her brother, stopped short of the house. The thatched straw roof had now almost disappeared. She could see flames dancing through the shattered windowpanes.

Yaroslaw sent Maria to knock on some of the neighbours' houses to get more help.

"Get help, get buckets, lots of buckets, go, go now," he instructed her firmly.

Many of the neighbours were soon up and out of their beds, racing to the house to help. One neighbour took Johanna to the village doctor. Not an official doctor, but someone who they often turned to for medical issues, to have her head wound taken care of.

The younger children were taken in by another neighbour. She kindly gave the youngsters a drink of warm milk to settle them and a warm blanket, telling them to try and get some rest.

Maria was frantically worried for her Mama and their lovely little home. Although Vasyl soon fell asleep, she couldn't bring herself to even close her eyes because of the thoughts bouncing around in her mind.

Yaroslaw and several of the men from the village, filled buckets with water from the well, passing them along a line of helpers towards the house in an to attempt to drown out the flames, but the fire had taken a firm hold and it was just impossible to extinguish.

The dark hours of the night passed, the morning sky slowly appearing. Easter Sunday, and the fire had finally begun to burn out to a simmer.

The exhausted men decided to let nature take over, knowing little else could be done now to save the house.

Yaroslaw, feeling both defeated and deflated, dragged his feet home. Johanna and the children stayed at the neighbour's house, managing just a few hours of fitful sleep.

As the sun rose, so did Johanna, feeling dizzy with concussion. She needed to see the house for herself. She wanted to see if they still had a place to call home.

Vasyl slept on, the horror and upset of the previous night catching up with him. Johanna left him with the neighbour. Unsure what state they would find their home in, she tried to protect him from the sadness and worry.

Maria rose from the sleepless bed to follow her Mama, linking an arm tightly through Johanna's. It was as much to steady her own shaky legs as to support her Mama, who's her head was wrapped in a bloodstained bandage.

Their stomachs churned as they entered the front yard, glancing around at the smouldering remains of a home that once was. They could hear Yaroslaw coughing abruptly from inside. He had been unable to sleep and wanted to see if he could salvage anything now daylight had arrived.

Johanna began to cry, sad heavy sobs, tears flooding over her pale cheeks. Maria had heard her Mama cry many times after Tato died, always in the next room or in the middle of the night, never in front of her or Vasyl. She had never seen the tears falling on her smooth beautiful face.

As they walked into the shuddering remains of the house, Yaroslaw turned around to face them. "There's very little left, Mama," he announced sadly.

Mama nodded in agreement as she scanned the room. The lingering smoke stung her eyes, causing a thickening to the lining of her throat and she began to cough. "The accordion?" she questioned.

"It's Gone Mama, it's gone." He quivered, holding back the tears. They each knew how much the accordion meant to Mama, to all of them. It held a childhood full of happy memories. His father's prized possession, which had been propped beside the fire where Tato left it.

Trying to contain her heavy sobbing, Johanna carefully stepped through the remains of the charred room and into the back of the house. Maria followed close behind, both holding a hand over their mouths to block out the thick choking smoke. The fire had raged throughout the rooms. There was little, if anything, that could be salvaged. The Easter basket had been scooped up into a dusting of ash. Its contents had disappeared.

With a huge wave of sadness and helplessness, Johanna left by the back of the house. Escaping into the fresh air. In a daze and bewildered motion, she wondered what on earth to do next.

Moving in a muted state, she headed into the outhouse. The chickens needed feeding, she realised, grabbing a tub of grain from the straw feed bag, she began scattering the grain around the yard like confetti, the chickens greedily pecking at the offerings oblivious to the previous night-times events that had taken place, it was just another day to them.

Yaroslaw followed Johanna out into the yard, concerned but unsure what he could say or do to make things better, something Mama had always been good at, it seemed. She always had a few positive words to share to make things seem better.

"Mama? Mama?" he questioned, unsure what he was asking, not sure what he could do, not knowing anything at all in this moment in time.

It had been a long time since he had opened his arms to his Mama, if he ever had. It had always been Johanna stealing cuddles from her eldest son. However, he thought this was maybe the answer to give at this moment. After all, there were no other answers he could think of at present.

Striding over to Mama, wrapping his strong arms around her shoulders, she collapsed into his hold, grateful for the comfort. Seconds later, a confused Maria joined the pair in the embrace. Each seemingly recharging their energy.

During the early morning, several villagers came to offer help, but in truth nothing could be done. The house was no longer a safe home, it couldn't be salvaged.

A couple of neighbours had thoughtfully brought the family some of their clothes to wear.

Leaving the burnt ruins behind and collecting Vasyl on the way, Yaroslaw took the family along to his home where the three of them managed to wash and change into clean clothing.

Putting their worries behind them for a short time the family strolled along to the village church to join the Easter service, the local priest blessing the Easter baskets with holy water.

Gossip had spread through the small village, each of the residents knowing about the fire and the priest gave a special blessing to the family as the service came to an end.

Johanna took up the kind offer to share an Easter meal with the neighbours from further down the lane. Feeling sad and gloomy, she really didn't want to be a part of the gathering, but realised the children would benefit from some joy out of the occasion.

The neighbour took in the small family for the following week, while arrangements were made for them to begin life in a new house. Matvijs extended family had several houses in the village and they were given use of one of the homes in exchange for the use of the land they currently owned. The new house had just a small pasture in comparison, but at least they had somewhere to live.

The family soon moved into the house and set up their new home.

***

Johanna was never the same again, after the bang on the head. She was continually zapped of all energy, often suffering dizzy spells and frequent nausea, whilst still suffering with her serious, previous, stomach pains

Several months passed and still there was no improvement.

She spent long hours laying on the bed, unable to rise and complete any chores.

Although Yaroslaw helped when he could, he and Anna had their own home to keep, their own fields to tend to and they had recently discovered Anna was expecting a baby, so spare time and energy was limited. Anna soon became resentful of his time spent helping others, even if it was his own family.

Neighbours rallied around as much as they could, helping to keep the children fed. Unfortunately, Johanna seemed to be wasting away before their eyes, with a drawn, gaunt greyness about her usual rosy face.

***

Arriving at the house, one fresh but bright autumn morning, with a warm pan of porridge for the family, a close neighbour noticed the curtains that hung down over the main window were still drawn, they were all early risers; it was in their nature, so this was a strange occurrence.

She let herself into the house, knowing the doors were never locked, entering the darkened front room. To the far side, she could see Johanna, the sweet beauty, motionless below a woollen blanket, laying upon a makeshift bed. She felt a calm chill in the air, the fire had burnt down. Walking towards the bed, she caught her breath with shock.

Johanna looked so peaceful, but she wasn't sleeping. At just thirty-nine years of age, the young mother had sadly passed away.

Quietly entering the room to the back of the house, she could see the children, Maria cradling Vasyl like a baby, snuggled together under the blankets, sleeping soundly. For now, she would leave them be, let them dream their pleasant dreams. They would have more than enough to deal with when they awoke.

Orphaned at such a young age. How would she break the news to them?

What would become of the children now?

Who would take care of them?

Once the children woke, the neighbour quickly ushered them outside to play in the fields, both grumbling somewhat that they hadn't yet eaten their porridge. The neighbour passed them each a pear that she had found sat on the ledge by the back window, soaking up the last of the autumn rays to ripen.

There was so much to be done, and the youngsters didn't need to be involved or be aware of the events until later, when they would return home hungry to find a house full of mourners and their precious Mama laid out on the kitchen table.

Life as they knew it had once again changed its pathway.

The following few days saw a stream of family members and neighbours calling to give their sympathy and blessings, each shedding heavy tears for the loss.

In the weeks that followed the funeral, Maria and Vasyl moved in with Yaroslaw and Anna.

It wasn't to be a happy time; the grieving youngsters weren't made to feel particularly welcome by Anna at their new home.

Yaroslaw was constantly busy, working in the fields, unaware of the ongoing difficulties arising in the house.

Although, he had already become aware of Anna's sharp tongue and her lack of sensitivity, he, as well as his siblings were grieving in their own private ways.

Anna begrudged having to take care of them both, however, Vasyl was younger and quieter than Maria and Anna found him easier to manage and easier to put upon. She just didn't care for Maria much at all, thought she had too many big ideas in her head and too much to say for herself. Anna would often send her to sleep in the freezing cold, dirty outhouse, out of her sight, with just the hay covered floor to provide her any warmth.

***

Within six months, Yaroslaw was enlisted for the army and sent away to fight for their country.

The lack of care given to youngsters sadly continued and the arrival of their new baby boy, Omelyan, soon put an immediate end to their stay.

Vasyl aged nine was temporarily taken in by an Auntie who lived close by in the neighbouring village, Nahoryany. The Auntie had several children of her own to care for. The home was overcrowded and, struggling for space and the ability to feed another mouth, she was insistent that she couldn't possibly take on two extra children. Young Vasyl could be useful to help on the land, she'd thought. At almost fourteen, Maria was older, she would cope better with life away from home, the Auntie convinced herself.

A reluctant Maria was taken away by the nuns to spend time in an orphanage in Zalischiki. Tears gathered in her eyes as she was separated from Vasyl. She promised him she would be back soon.

Leaving behind her worried little brother was the most difficult situation for her, but she needed to stay strong for him.

"I will always take care of you," she promised. "I will be back soon," she whispered into his ear as bent down to hug him a goodbye.

Tears ran down her trembling cheeks as she left the village, leaving behind all she knew of life. Glancing down the lane for one last time, she could picture Mama smiling brightly, still feeling the warmth of her mother's arms around her. An image that would stay trapped in her mind forever, encouraging her to become a strong young woman just like her Mama had taught her to be. She vowed to herself that she wouldn't allow anyone or anything in life to bring her down.

The orphanage, an ancient stone convent building, was enormous. Maria hesitated as she followed behind the sister, up the high steps that led to the huge arched doorway entrance and into the cold, darkened hallway. She wrapped her arms tightly around chest, as nervous shivers ran through her body. Stepping inside, the silent sister reached around Maria and closed the solid door, turning a key in the lock. This startled Maria. Back home in the village, they had a lock on the front door, although she knew a key hung on a hook by the side of the door, she couldn't remember it ever needing to be used.

The shivers continued through her body, trembling in her stomach, shaking at her hands and creating a wobbly sensation in her legs. She tried to tell herself to be calm, stay strong, but she really didn't know what to expect here in these new surroundings and the silence of the unwelcoming nun was doing nothing to put her at ease.

Ordering Maria to remain where she was standing, the sister walked over to a large black, glossy door and knocked twice. She then turned the brass doorknob and entered the room behind it, closing the door as she disappeared within.

Maria waited quietly, fighting the urge to cough and clear her throat of the bee's wax and pine scent that had filled her senses as she tried to calm her breathing.

The clattering of footsteps interrupted the silence. She glanced along the corridor leading off the entrance hallway. Several nuns, in their long floor sweeping tunics, sauntered along, their veils perfectly positioned on their heads. Their faces were sour and serious. None of them took any notice of Maria, as though she was concealed from their sight.

Eventually, the large door re-opened. Out stepped a large, rounded Mother Superior. She glared over the gold-rimmed glasses that were neatly perched near the edge of her nose, then stood to one side of the doorway and pointed her finger, gesturing Maria to enter the room.

Inside was a huge oak desk littered with stacks of folders and piles of paper on the top, leaving just a small space free for the empty cup and saucer that sat in it. A comfortable looking leather seat behind the desk was soon occupied by the hefty frame of the Mother Superior.

Maria stood by the silent nun, waiting to maybe answer any questions or be given any information. Apart from confirming her name, neither happened. The Head of the nunnery kept her expression fixed as she read the letter she held in her hand. Placing it onto the stack of paperwork once she had finished reading, she glared at Maria.

"We have no trouble here. We have rules to follow. If they are broken, there will be consequences, do you understand?" she questioned in the Ukrainian language.

"Tak," Maria returned in confirmation.

"Sister Veronika will show you to your room," she informed, nodding her head towards the nun.

The brief, unfriendly introduction was over. Sister Veronika opened the door. She strode off ahead and Maria once again followed, pulling the heavy door to a close behind her. She quickened her pace to catch up with Sister Veronika, realising her trembling body had eased slightly.

The nun took the lead up the beautiful, winding staircase, Maria's hand smoothed over the gleaming wooden banister rail as she made her way to the top of the highly polished stairs. Reaching the final steps, Maria looked around. Apart from four doorways, the whitewashed walls were bare, stark, empty of any framed paintings, with no decoration of homely touches.

Entering the bedroom ahead, Maria paused to take in her surroundings. A long, cold space with huge windows to the far end, which allowed one side of the room its daylight. The edges of the cold, wooden floor lined with cramped rows of small beds. Each of them with perfectly smooth and neatly fitted sheets upon them, a blanket folded and placed at the end. All the beds had a small bedside cupboard to one side. There was nothing else to see in the room.

It was barren, it had been less than an hour since Maria had arrived and she was already convinced, this place wasn't a home, it was completely devoid of life. There was not a toy or childlike item to be found. Only the hundreds of children convinced her that this was an orphanage.

Over the following days, Maria soon met the other girls in her dormitory. They were all aged between twelve and fifteen. The other bedrooms were the sleeping quarters for other girls of different age groups. The boys were apparently housed in a separate adjoining part of the building, although they were only seen occasionally through the window as they crossed the large yard area to join mass.

Maria had thought maybe she would make some friends, living so closely with the others, but the other girls seemed dreary and unhappy. There was no laughter or smiles to be found. The children's faces as they went about their daily routines were joyless, devoid of any happiness.

It was during the night, after lights-out, that Maria, amongst others, dared to whisper, and even then, only to the person in the next bed. They were scared that the nuns may be listening and fix a punishment for them not going to sleep. Idle chatter was forbidden, as were most things. Maria had discovered many rules. These rules made it difficult to feel any control over her life.

The nuns could really be quite cruel, they had a very sharp, strict manner about them. Rules were set. Many instructions and chores were given out and these were to be abided by without any questions or hesitation.

Maria didn't care much for the house rules, or the way in which they were set, but she was happy to earn her keep, glad to have food in her stomach and a warm bed to sleep in at the end of each day.

Maria spent many months in the care of the nuns, becoming more and more disgusted by the manner of the sisters, hating how small and worthless they could make her feel. She wanted to be with Vasyl, she needed to check he was doing well. She craved the familiarity and safety of the village and wanted so much to be back at her family home.

One day, she awoke feeling more homesick than ever before. She had decided whilst eating the breakfast offerings of thick tasteless porridge, that she'd had enough of this cruel routine, so, instead of heading towards the laundry to start her work shift, she quickly sneaked back along the highly polished floor to the dormitory to collect her few personal belongings.

Thankfully, the door to the garden had been left ajar, letting in a cold gust of late autumn air. Hurrying outside, she paced along the gravelled pathway which led along the side of the huge, grey, eerie looking stone building.

Rushing across the courtyard, her feet pounding as she passed the line of apple trees rustling in the breeze. Swathed in greens and reds, the odd late ripening fruit clung to its branches. These were treasures that only the nuns could pick. They were too precious for the mouths of mere orphans. Without giving it too much thought Maria stopped, quickly checking behind her for prying eyes; nobody was there. She grabbed at a branch, pulling it down towards her and twisted at the fruit, snapping it off the branch. She placed two beautifully ripe, green apples into her apron pockets as she hurried along through the tall iron gates that lead onto the cobbles of the main street. These would be a lovely treat for Vasyl and herself when she reached home.

It was as easy as that. Nobody came chasing after her as she'd expected. Nobody seemed to care. To them she was just another parentless child she thought, nobody would miss her.

Leaving the orphanage behind her, she sped up her step and headed home, taking the long, long, walk back to the village.

She didn't have a plan. She didn't even know her way home. She didn't know if she would be in any trouble for leaving the orphanage. She just knew she needed to be at home and taking care of her young brother.

Her journey completed, she finally arrived some six or seven hours later. She called over to Auntie's house to check that Vasyl was alright.

The Aunt was fuming with Maria for leaving the orphanage. It had been a struggle for her with an extra mouth to feed. Feeding Maria as well would be an impossible ask. She had seven children of her own to take care of and she just wasn't prepared or able to take on more.

Vasyl had been unhappy at Auntie's without his sister beside him, he had been given a lot of chores to earn his keep, too many for a youngster. His face lit up when he saw Maria, he was overjoyed to have her back in his life.

***

The two children, although still young, moved back into the family home alone. Left to fend for themselves.

They hadn't lived there, in the new house for long before Mama had passed away. It hadn't felt like home to them, not like the comfortable house full of pleasant memories that had burnt.

There hadn't been anyone working the pasture since the death of her Mama, the dry crops and empty ground told her so. The young pair spent several days hunting for any surviving crops they could find. Digging for potatoes was seemingly their only option. Thankfully, their prayers were answered, and by the end of the following day, they had managed to collect a small sack full. There was little else to be found and with the freezing winter season fast approaching, there was nothing left to be done on the land to provide instant food for their hungry stomachs.

Water and potatoes would be their menu for the coming months. Hopefully they would be able to forage for more food before winter arrived.

Scrubbing the soil from the potatoes, Maria sent Vasyl outside to find a stock of wood. The house was so bitterly cold, they needed to collect a good supply of kindling to warm them through. The siblings decided to keep to just the main room, creating a makeshift bed there.

***

It was a long and freezing cold winter. The children, struggling to keep warm, would wrap up the best they could and venture out into the village on the hunt for wood, returning with ice covered branches that would hopefully dry out ready for burning.

Their hunger was endless, the potatoes and peelings had long since been eaten and with no food to be found, the pair would head into the fields on the hunt for anything that could ease the hunger pains in their stomachs. Searching for berries, mushrooms, anything that could be eaten raw or made into a soup. The siblings would visit the village to attend the church service, praying to God for his help. Occasionally, a neighbour would take pity on the orphaned pair and kindly provide them with a small food offering. This wasn't a regular gift to rely on.

The deep snow had arrived in November and hadn't begun to show signs of thawing until the following March. Spring finally arrived, bursting a symphony of beauty and with it an end to the long, frozen days.

Asking around, Maria had managed to find a small job working for the local priest and his wife in the next village. Her duties were to take on cleaning in their home and washing their laundry by the stream.

Life had begun to improve slightly since the winter, with an increase of food and energy.

***

The first day of May 1942, was an early start. As the beautiful, glowing sun rose, Maria left Vasyl at home whilst she went out to work her morning shift.

Today the Priest's wife had left a pile of dirty garments for Maria to wash. Carrying them down to the nearby stream, Maria scrubbed…

By early afternoon, her work for the day was complete and she leisurely made the walk back home, grateful to be carrying a freshly baked loaf of bread and a handful of fresh, homegrown vegetables that the priest's wife had given her as payment for her completed work.

An elderly man she knew of from the village was slowly heading towards her. He bent over his wooden walking stick for support as he came to a halt on the lane and looked over towards Maria.

"Be careful, the Germans are here," he announced in a muttered manner before he began his crawl again.

Panic rushed through Maria.

"Stay safe," he advised, not looking back.

In a shocked silent state, she rushed ahead towards the centre of the village. As she reached the turn in the road, she could hear the loud rumble of the huge trucks ahead. A dozen or so armed German soldiers were strutting and yelling along the lane, some pushing and pulling aggressively at the frightened young peasants and ordering them onto the cattle trucks.

Maria froze with fright and panic. Trying to make sense of the scene erupting before her. The moment had come, *her time*, she thought, knowing it would happen one day soon. It had only been a matter of fate. Gossip had passed through the villagers over the last couple of weeks. The Germans were arriving in the neighbouring villages daily, rounding up young peasants, taking them to camps for forced labour.

"Get yourself ready, girl," spat a soldier as he neared Maria. "Now! Hurry! Get yourself ready and get on the truck. Don't make me come and find you!" he warned with a touch of his rifle.

She had just turned sixteen this spring, leaving her little option but to be taken for forced labour. Life was so tough. Maria was thinking it might be a good thing to go, then hopefully the family would have to take in Vasyl and take good care of him. She also thought naively that maybe the Germans would be a welcome change to brutal Stalin.

Maria sprinted with a matter of urgency to their house, but Vasyl was nowhere to be seen. Placing the loaf and vegetables down on the chair by the fire grate, she rushed down towards to edge of the village to her Aunty's house. Racing in through the open front door, she announced her news.

"They're taking me away, the Germans are here, they're taking me away!" she panicked, trying to catch her breath.

Maria was surprised to note the Auntie looked unexpectantly upset. She had been stirring a large metal pot of broth and placed the ladle down beside it, wiping her hands on her apron as she tried to find words of comfort for the young girl she had let down. But she couldn't.

"I can't find Vasyl. I need to tell him I'm going away, and I want to say goodbye," Maria rushed.

"He is out walking my cow. Maybe he will be in the meadow," replied Auntie calmly.

Maria was so annoyed; how could she send the boy out to walk the cow when the Germans were looming? She'd told him to stay at home and be safe. Did this happen every day when she had gone to work?

Maria turned abruptly to leave the house.

"Here, quickly, let me make you some food to take on your journey," Auntie offered with a prickle of conscience.

Rage came over Maria. "No!" she spat. "We needed food over the winter when we were starving and you didn't offer us any, so I certainly don't want it now." The anger welled up heavy in her chest.

Maria turned her back furiously on her auntie and rushed out of the house, wondering where on earth Vasyl could be with the cow. She had strictly told him to stay in the house until she returned from work. Gone were the days of wondering in the village or fields, with the Germans' imminent arrival.

"Stay close to home," she had constantly instructed him each day.

There wasn't any time to start worrying or searching around for her brother, but she felt frantic. The Germans were waiting, and she didn't want to experience their angry impatience or the consequences that may come of her hesitance.

Knowing nothing of what lay ahead, she somehow believed that life surely couldn't be any worse.

Vasyl had been out secretively playing in the orchard, having become bored of sitting inside the house alone waiting for his sister to return. As he did most days, he had called around to Aunty's house to walk her cow, a chore he had quite enjoyed doing when Maria had been away in the orphanage.

He had heard the panic rising in the village. From the far corner of the pasture, he could see onto the main lane that entered the village. His frightened eyes bearing a silent witness from the meadow.

He paused, holding tightly to the rope around the cow's huge neck. Standing quietly still, watching as people were being pushed by the soldiers onto a cattle truck, not having a clue where they were heading, he just knew that if the Germans were taking them, it wasn't good.

The cattle truck set off crawling down the lane, as if in search of more occupants to fill the small gaps left on board.

Panic rose from inside him as he spotted the familiar face through the trees. In the distance, sat up high, searching all around her, was Maria.

What was she doing on the truck?

Who was she looking for?

He wanted to scream out loud to his sister. 'I'm here, Maria, I'm here,' instead he winced and muttered a cry.

Tears flooded his eyes, blinking to clear his view as the truck revved further along the lane and began leaving the village.

Leaving the cow munching happily on the long grass, he raced across the ground. He lurched forward onto the lane after the crowded cattle truck. His frightened legs wouldn't carry him at the speed of the huge metal cased vehicle.

As the truck reached the bridge, Maria looked back towards the village. She saw her baby brother by the lane side. Sadness swept over her. With a pang of guilt, she turned away, focusing her eyes on the road ahead. There was nothing she could do to ease his pain or her own for that matter. Little did she know that she was leaving behind an entire life.

As the truck went over the bridge and headed out of the village, Vasyl had to admit defeat. His shaking, wobbly legs dropping him to the ground. His heart thumping hard through his chest. Huge tears erupted, streaming endlessly down his face. The emptiness he felt smothered him.

What would he do without his protector?

Where would she be taken?

What would they do without each other?

He sat for a short while, looking down the empty dirt track, the roar of the engine and yells of the soldiers replaced by an eerie silence. Even the birds had gone quiet. Maria wasn't going to return, she had been taken away, his most precious possession, taken away from him and all he knew so abruptly.

Forgetting all about the cow, he slowly dragged his feet over to Anna's house. Yaroslaw was still away with the army, fighting for their country's freedom. As an eleven-year-old boy, he was unsure what exactly this meant. Maria had told him about the war, about the Germans, but she had protected him from any horrific details she had heard rumoured.

"She's gone, Maria's gone, they've taken My Maria," he wept as Anna opened the door, huge tears swelling his throat. His eyes were puffy and red rimmed. He had never felt so alone, so empty, totally devastated.

The family house Maria left behind

Marias Austrian documents

8
Graz -Austria

Taking Maria further away from her place of home in Ukraine, the dreadful, lengthy journey was one spent in several horrendously packed vehicles. Initially groups of around sixty people, both men and women were crammed into extremely overcrowded cattle trucks.

Long, long hours passed with little or no space for them to sit, let alone lie down or stretch out their legs. Only the glimmers of daylight gave them an idea of time spent along the journey.

The group were then forced onto a filthy cattle train.

Crammed into the darkened wagons with only a few slits in the wall panels to allow any chance of light or fresh air.

The train would stop frequently to pick up additional forced labourers. Adding more hours to the already painful journey.

In an attempt to keep their spirits up and quench some time, many in the group would sing patriotic songs. Others would pray together. Maria felt the need to take part in both the singing and praying. Both passed the time and made her feel a little less anxious.

As the singing ended, the mumbling of miserable moans returned to fill the musty air. Maria found a space on the floor, huddled between a large bearded, stale smelling man and a hysterical woman whose body trembled through her tears. There was no chatting, no laughter in the misery.

There was slight relief as the evening began to arrive. The train would come to a halt and each member of the group were allowed to disembark for a short time, they weren't allowed to venture far, but it gave them to chance to stretch their legs or empty their bladders if they had managed to hold it in or hadn't found a space to crouch in the carriage. At these brief stop offs, the group were provided with a small ration of bread and a mug of water.

The last day of the route was a day of drop offs, passengers released at towns close to their places of new employment. Several uncomfortable, sleepless days of travel had passed before the journey finally came to an end for Maria and her group of fellow workers.

The relief however, was short lived.

The groups arrival in Graz was one of misery. No one welcomed them. The first couple of months were spent in a holding camp, a cold and empty deteriorated school building. A dark and dim place, damp and unpleasant. Maria's hopes and spirits were completely deflated.

***

Endless days were spent sitting around, the memories of what she'd left behind leaving a hollow pain in her chest. They ate nothing but a small daily ration of stale bread and a mug of watery, tasteless broth and the daily role call sent just half a dozen people to their new employment each day.

The process felt endless until Maria's name was eventually called.

She was collected by Mr Pignitter, an older gentleman, smartly dressed in a nut-brown three-piece suit. A black felt hat perched on his head, not the style of dress Maria had ever seen. His greying moustache turned up at the ends as he smiled gently towards Maria.

She felt totally at ease as they drove away, leaving the main town centre and heading towards the countryside. The windows wound down slightly, letting in a gentle breeze and easing the strong aroma of pipe tobacco from the vehicle. The dark green farm truck rumbling at every turn on the road, breaking the silence that was trapped between the driver and his passenger, Maria, with their language barrier.

The journey thankfully wasn't too long, and Mr Pignitter was soon swerving the truck down a long, dusty track. Maria looked ahead in amazement. It was the first time in months she had been able to take in the fresh air and this beautiful, mountainous place had plenty of it. She gasped as she looked around her. A mass of fields, endless neat rows of healthy crops, fields of cows munching at the long green grass, glimmering blue skies above. She instantly felt at home.

Up ahead of them stood a beautiful, huge white house, surrounded by large trees and the prettiest of flowers in an array of colours. Wooden window boxes sat on the sills, bursting further colourful mixes of bloom. A stunning wooden balcony clung to the upper rooms of the building. She had never seen anything quite like it.

Passing several outhouse farm buildings, the truck pulled to a stop outside the main home. To the front of the house, a small table perched on the gravelled area. Seated around it was a young gentleman, wearing a pair of grey overalls that had been unbuttoned at the top and hung loosely by his waist, revealing an olive-green shirt.

Next to him, an older lady sat, a light blue headscarf upon her head, an apron covering the checked material of her dress. The lady was pouring a bottle of what looked like lemon juice into a tall glass and handing it to a pretty little girl of five or six years old who stood beside her. Each of them stood as the truck pulled up and they started to walk over in its direction. Maria stayed seated inside the vehicle, unsure if she should be leaving the truck.

Mr Pignitter walked around to the passenger side of the truck and opened the door. "Come," he instructed her politely, his welcoming smile, easing her nerves slightly.

Stepping down from the truck, Maria was face to face with these new people. Maria knew only the odd word in German, so she was relieved when the family immediately greeted her with handshakes and friendly smiles, breaking her sense of silence.

First, she was introduced to the lady of the farm, Mrs Pignitter, an older woman, her grey hair fastened tightly into bun on top of her head. Stood beside her was their grown up son Kirt, his rough working hands shook Maria's to greet her. The cute little girl shyly hung onto her father's overalls, trying not to be seen but not wanting to miss out on the arrival of their new visitor.

The Pignitter Family Home

The Pignitter Family

"Caecilia, say hello to Maria," Mrs Pignitter requested of her granddaughter, swirling the girl's blond curls around her fingers.

The small girl just smiled coyly.

***

The family soon embraced Maria as part of their household, playfully renaming her Mitzy. Allowing her to share their beautiful home, their mealtimes and their family time, trusting her as one of them. Giving her a comfortable bed in a room of her own, Maria couldn't have been made more welcome.

Maria worked hard on the farm, happily spending long days in the fields tending to the crops, in the yard feeding the animals and cleaning the cattle sheds, in any way that was asked of her. She worked amongst several other farm workers, mainly family members, and although the work could be tough, especially in the harsh winters, she thoroughly enjoyed being part of this family and earning her keep.

Occasionally at the weekends, the family would invite Maria to join them at a dance in the local village hall or out into town for a shopping trip. Maria was more than happy to attend these journeys out and began to feel a real part of the community, grateful for the kindness offered by the Pignitter family.

Maria made quite a few good friends in the village on these outings, fellow Ukrainians as well as Austrian locals. Mostly those who found themselves in the same position as her, taken away from their homes, trying to learn this new language and make the best out of the situation as they could. Sadly, many weren't as fortunate as Maria to find comfort and a welcome from their new employers.

When Maria had some free time away from working, she began to venture out from the farmhouse, going for walks and meeting with her new friends. She learnt enough words from this new language to get by and although her employment merely covered her with board and food, the Pignitters obligingly provided Maria with a small amount of money for these outings.

Several carefree months had passed, but the war hadn't ended and when the Russians arrived, everyone's frayed nerves were put on a sharp edge, as curfews were installed.

The days of singing her beautiful folk songs whilst working in the fields had to stop. The family were frightened for Maria's safety. Mrs Pignitter especially, had seen Maria as a daughter, cared for her deeply and didn't want any harm to come to her.

One warm April morning Mrs Pignitter wondered over into the fields with Caecilia by her side. Maria and another worker were busy planting potatoes. As she became closer to the pair, Mrs Pignitter froze. She was so cross and upset with what she could hear she started shouting at Maria. Maria was stunned. She had never heard Mrs Pignitter shout, least of all at her.

"Na, Na Mitzy!!!" she blurted, yelling that Maria mustn't sing. "If they hear you, they will know you are Ukrainian. No more singing Maria, no more!" she repeated.

Maria understood the danger, but was disappointed, after all, singing was a huge part of her. How could she not sing.

As Mrs Pignitter walked away, feeling a little guilty at being so abrupt but having said her piece. Maria pulled a funny face for the little girl's benefit, making Caecilia giggle by her grandmother's side, finding the whole situation enormously funny.

Sitting down with the family for the evening meal later that day. Maria knew something big was about to be discussed. Kirt had placed Caecilia into bed early tonight so they could speak openly without little ears listening.

Dangerous situations were lurking, Kirt stated, they needed Mitzy to stay safe or they would all be in danger.

"If you are approached on the farm or in the fields, you must pretend you can't hear, pretend that you are mute. If they try to speak to you must be silent. If you open your mouth, they will know you are Ukrainian," suggested Mr Pignitter.

"As much as everyone loves to hear you sing, Mitzy, this must be an end to the singing, do you understand?" questioned Mrs Pignitter.

"The day for your beautiful singing will return one day, I promise you Mitzy." She smiled warmly towards Maria.

Maria agreed to all the requests from the family. She was concerned for her own safety, and she certainly didn't want to put any of them in any danger. They had all been so kind to her.

After they had finished the meal, the men moved into the next room to play a card game. Maria helped Mrs Pignitter clear away the dishes from the table and set to washing the plates and cutlery in the kitchen.

Maria didn't often find the opportunity to speak to Mrs Pignitter alone, as little Caecilia was always by her grandmother's side. As far as she understood, the little girl's mother had passed away, although any details were unknown to Maria.

The Pignitters also had a daughter, however Maria had only met her once during her stay, when she had visited with her two young children and her husband. It had been a rare and short visit, although Maria couldn't understand why. Maybe they lived too far away. It was never questioned.

Picking up a towel, Maria began wiping dry the plates. She attempted to explain her worries to Mrs Pignitter. Using a little Ukrainian and some of the German language she had learned since leaving home. Unable to find such horrific words.

A close friend of hers from the nearby village had been violently raped by a Russian soldier. As if this ordeal wasn't bad enough for the poor girl, she had needed help to make herself lose the baby. The girl had shared her nightmare with Maria and couple of other close friends, to warn them of the dangers to themselves. She had told the friends not to go alone to any dances in the village, told them not to leave the safety of their housing when looking nice or clean. She had herself, stopped washing or brushing her own hair, terrified to look too good to the Russians. Believing if she looked undesirable, the soldiers wouldn't bother to look at her.

Mrs Pignitter was appalled by the story. Maria wouldn't divulge the friend's name, having been told in confidence, but assured her that the girl was well and that she was in a house that was as safe as could be.

Mrs Pignitter took the drying cloth from Maria's hands, placing it on the worktop. She sat her down on the stool by the kitchen window and gathered her in her arms. It had been a long time since Maria had felt so cared for. She appreciated the warm embrace being offered.

Mrs Pignitter warned Maria, she must stay by the farm, she mustn't go out of the farmyard alone. If she wanted to meet up with her friends, then one of the family would drive her into the village.

"Never take any chances, Mitzy, never!" she pleaded.

***

Life on the farm continued much as before, with each of them taking a little extra care to look out for each other.

Late one afternoon Maria was busy bringing the goats in from the field, herding them from behind with a branch she had picked up along the way and directing them across the yard towards the cattle shed. As she looked back across the yard to check there were no strays, she noticed a lone parachutist drifting across the edge of the field.

The parachute caught on the branches of a tree as he descended, and the airman was trapped.

Maria raced across the yard to the farmhouse. Kirt and his father had just gone inside. "Komm, Komm und hilf," she yelled for help into the doorway, aware that she still had her muddy boots on her feet and she couldn't dare to step inside onto Mrs Pignitter clean floor. "Hilf," she cried out for help.

Within seconds Kirt was rushing towards the door, followed closely behind by both Mr and Mrs Pignitter, worried expressions covered their faces.

Maria pointed to the field, the parachutist hanging from the highest branch, tangled in the larch tree. They all rushed over to the airman. Cutting at the cords with his penknife, Kirt released him and they all helped him down carefully and onto the floor below.

Carrying him to one of the barns, they could see by his uniform he was an English serviceman. A worried look upon his pale face, his hands shook as he sat down but he seemed to calm down as Mrs Pignitter saw to the cuts on his forehead, bathing them in some warm water, whilst sending Maria into the house to get a bowl of stew and a slice of bread for the unexpected arrival.

Neither could understand the other's language to ask any questions, however the, "Thank you," was obvious in appreciation of food received. The airman was bedded down on the hay for a night in the barn and given a woollen blanket and cup of warm tea.

A worried Mr Pignitter hastily drove into town to inform the officials of their cattle shed resident.

At dawn the following morning, the officials arrived at the farm, the airman was collected swiftly and taken away.

The village was becoming busy with troops, making for a constant unease. Soldiers prowled everywhere, threatening guns by their sides.

Up early one crisp Sunday morning, Maria accompanied Mr and Mrs Pignitter on a stroll. The family hadn't left the farm in quite a few weeks and had thought it would be a good idea to take in some fresh air and stretch their legs. They weren't planning to venture too far away, just far enough to feel the benefit of the time away from the farmhouse.

Along the way Maria spent time picking some wildflowers from the roadside, placing them carefully into a pretty and colourful bunch. She would place them into one of Mrs Pignitters glass vases on their return to brighten up the table in the dining room. Maria felt relaxed, which was an unusual feeling to her in the last few months, a feeling that she really appreciated having, if even for just one morning.

They walked blissfully along the lane that ran down the side of the farmland into the village. Peace followed them as they strolled along, listening intently to the birds singing sweetly.

Reaching the end of the lane, they arrived at the crossroads. Maria hadn't been able to attend the church service recently. Mrs Pignitter knew how much Maria needed religion in her life, knew how disappointed she had been lately to miss the church services. Maybe they could all attend today, she had thought as they arrived at the fork in the road. Suddenly, out of nowhere, an unshaven but smartly dressed man began racing towards them, catching them all off guard. They stood startled by the stone wall to the side of the gravelled pathway. The stubbly red-faced man rushed on by them, no hesitation, certainly no stopping. He looked petrified.

As he rushed past, his breath heavy with panic, he spoke briefly to inform them. "Go home, go straight home, don't go down there, get out of here!" He stormed, turning his head slightly towards them as he raced away.

Within seconds he was just a small figure in the distance as he left the lane and sprinted into the forest by the wayside.

Mr Pignitter grabbed at his wife's arm in his and reached out a hand to Maria. They were all startled and unsure of what had just taken place however, they knew life was totally unpredictable and no chances should be taken, especially in recent months.

None of them had time to gather their thoughts, instinct made each of them begin the hasty escape from whatever was happening further down the lane, at this moment they didn't need to know what it was they were hastily removing themselves from, they just needed to do it and do it fast.

The following day they heard news from the village that the Church along that lane had been set on fire. The parishioners, of mainly Ukrainian folk, were trapped inside the building with no way to escape the huge flames. Just a pile of smouldering rubble remained. Life was becoming even more frightening.

Maria couldn't settle that evening, she lay in the bed, unable to ease the tightness in chest, her heart pounding so fierce and fast she thought it may never slow down. She struggled to ignore what had taken place at the church. She could have easily been one of those victims who were, no doubt, innocently praying to their god for peace and an end to the fighting. Someone had been looking over her, protecting her and keeping her safe. Whoever this angel was, she would be eternally grateful.

***

One warm, balmy evening Maria was out for a stroll around the farm after her evening meal. She had taken the farm dog with her for company and protection, as she thought.

The dog suddenly ran off from Maria, pounding across the side field, chasing a rabbit. She was careful not to shout too loud for the dog to return, not wanting to attract any unwanted attention. She raced after it, across the long grass, scanning in all directions for movement of the animal. Maria eventually found the dog, but having lost track of time, she began heading back towards the farm.

Walking along the back lane, she noticed a group of three soldiers approaching. It was too late to turn or run, they had already seen her and were striding towards her at speed. Their heavy boots pounded with delight at discovering somebody out after curfew and not just somebody but a lone young woman. Maria couldn't see anyone else around. Her solitary position had made her their target.

The soldiers' glances were most intimidating as they looked Maria closely up and down. Smirks upon their faces, they shouted that she was out after curfew.

One of the soldiers moved to the side of the lane and leaned against the stone wall, reaching into his pocket he took out a box of cigarettes, taking in a huge inhale as he lit his tobacco fix. He seemed uninterested in what was going on around him. This was his chance for a break maybe. Maybe he had seen it all before. He didn't need to be witness.

However, the other two soldiers seemed intent on being mean and showing their authority.

"Girl, papers? Where are your papers? Documents?" the youngest looking soldier began shouting.

Maria froze, she had only come outside to stretch her legs and get some fresh air before heading to bed for the night, she didn't have any documents with her, she was too frightened to open her mouth for fear of giving away who she was, where she was from or where she was staying.

"Hey, Girl, speak," he spat as he came up face to face with Maria. When he came close, the dog by Maria's side began barking frantically, making the young soldier jump out of his skin. *He isn't so tough looking now*, thought

Maria.

The older soldier by his side began laughing as did the resting soldier, enjoying puffing away on his cigarette. Annoyed and embarrassed by his own weakness and by the dog continuing to bark, he raised his gun and quickly aimed at the animal.

The incident was over in seconds, but the pounding in Maria's chest remained, echoing the gunshot. The heartless soldier had shot the dog. A high-pitched whine came before a brief twitching and the dog lay still, motionless on the dark stained gravel. Without a care the young soldier turned and began to crunch away his heavy feet.

Maria was frozen to the spot. As the group of soldiers began heading away, taking up the pace once more in their solid boots, Maria remained stuck in her shoes, too terrified to move. She watched with relief as they started to leave. She could hear them muttering between themselves, a short distance away and the young solider turned towards her. Lifting his rifle, he aimed the gun towards a startled Maria.

Her heart pounded, throbbing as though it may jump out of her chest, her breathing became heavy. In a rush to complete his mission, he fired. With no real care or attention to his target, several shots were fired from the distance between them, two of the rounds bouncing of the dry ground by Maria, leaving a cloud of dust rising.

The third bullet had hit Maria in the leg.

Instantly she dropped to the ground. The tremendous pain of the bullets impact was soon replaced by a hot, sharp tingling. Lay on the floor in complete shock, blood pounding in her ears, she froze her body, too overwhelmed with the horror to move, she pretended to be dead, her heart raced wondering what might happen to her next. She could hear from the distance the soldiers were sneering and chuckling as they strolled off, leaving Maria and the dog by the lane side. Maria struggled to lie still, crying inside as the pain in her lower leg seared through her bone, causing a shudder within.

She let quite some time pass, waiting for the sound of the footsteps to disappear, giving herself time to regain her composure, before she dared to lift her head to check that she was alone. Looking down at her leg, she saw the gush of blood causing the warm sticky puddle that she lay in. Grabbing at her leg to stop the bleeding, she looked around her for the dog. It was too late. The dog was already dead. Hobbling as fast as she could, she made her way back to the farm, struggling as she carried the beloved animal in her arms.

She was soon approaching the farmyard. Drawing near the gates, her heart fluttered at the welcoming sight ahead. The door to the farmhouse was open, a lantern lighting the entrance, as the family gathered, concerned for the whereabouts of Mitzy so late in the evening. She couldn't have felt more relieved to be back to safety, back into the caring arms of Mrs Pignitter.

This frightening incident sadly wasn't to be the last.

Realising conditions were not going to ease anytime soon, the Pignitters had been discussing thoughts between them for if or when the Russians came onto their property. How or where would they hide Mitzy. Later that evening the family gathered, Mitzy included, to discuss their plans.

Before long, the plans were put into place.

The village had been a hive of activity, not with residents, however. Most of those had taken refuge inside their homes, not wanting to cause any aggravation, not wanting to draw attention to themselves amongst the dozens of soldiers arriving daily.

The change of uniform was hard to keep track of as the Russians overtook the Germans in position. The following days could see this in reverse. People were unsure what was about to happen, but each of them had a feeling a storm was brewing.

The Pignitters had devised a plan, together with Maria, in case they received unwelcome visitors to the farm. The plan seemed unthinkable, but necessary. Each of them knew what would happen, who would do what and when, but they all hoped with all their hearts that they wouldn't need to put the actions into practice.

After the shooting, Maria didn't venture from the farm. Mrs Pignitter had her helping around the farmhouse and taking care of Caecilia a little more lately, anything to keep her out of sight.

The dark nights began to draw in and on one of these evenings the family was about to settle at the dining table for their evening meal, when a roar of voices began approaching through the gates. Kirt had heard them first and peered out of the window to see what the commotion was. Horrified to see half a dozen soldiers pacing over towards the farmyard.

"They're here, the Russian brutes are here," he announced, his words echoing around the house. The relaxed, smooth actions of the house became frantic as they all rushed to take their place.

Sadly, they were left with little choice. The plan had to be put into action, sooner than they had all anticipated. Maria attempted to stay rational as she moved. She knew she had to keep a cool head. But feeling panic rising through her body, she headed nervously towards the fire grate in the main sitting room. Thankfully the evening fire hadn't yet been lit.

She placed the silencing piece of linen into her own mouth. Grabbing at Maria, Kirt, without any option, forcefully shoved her up the chimney. Her bare feet gripped the soot-stained brick sides as she tried to push herself further out of sight. Her legs shook, as they trembled. She had a strange feeling, like she was empty of any muscle and she was unsure how long she would be able to stay in this position.

Mr Pignitter hovered close by the front door, awaiting the knock, as was his place in the plan; keen to get this visit over as quickly as possible. Mrs Pignitter sat by the fire grate, picking up her sewing and placing it on her lap, to give a serine picture of innocence to the family, who at that moment felt anything but calm.

Thudding erupted as a soldier's firm fist began hammering on the door. Impatience proved to be his manner as he began shouting to those inside the farmhouse.

"Oun, oun nov," he began repeating, instructing them fiercely to open the door.

Mr Pignitter took in a deep breath, in readiness to deal with this nightmare, he was just a couple of steps from the door, however not close enough. The door was abruptly forced open from outside as the aggressive, irritable serviceman barged his way in, followed closely by the group of militaries.

The angry nightmare began. They had been informed that the family were keeping a Ukrainian in the household. This Ukrainian was to be found.

As Maria clung terrified, trying to steady her fast breathing in the darkness of the small brick space, she could hear the chaos erupting in the room below. The family, including little Caecilia, who was now nestled securely in the apron of her grandmother's arms, were forced at gunpoint to stand and face the wall. The deranged beasts ransacked the house, turning over heavy furniture, shooting manically at the beds and sofas, rounds blasted anywhere the Ukrainian might be hidden. They were all over the house, checking every room, every cupboard, shooting, shooting, shooting. Two of them returned from the barns, each with a pitchfork in their hands.

"Nein," they advised the officer in charge the person hadn't yet been found.

They were running out of hideouts, the house had been trashed, furniture lay on its side, vases and ornaments had been smashed, family photos had been ripped from the walls, slung across the floor needlessly. The two began to join in the hunt, stabbing their pitchforks into the bottom of the foam settees, turning them into sieves as the prongs were dug in again and again. The family could only imagine the disruption created in their beautiful home; eyes fixated on patterns in the wallpaper as they dared not see the goings on.

One of the pitchfork soldiers walked over to the fire. Feeling defeated in the search, he found a last stab of anger welling up inside him and he rammed the pitchfork up the chimney. Maria bit down hard on the linen as a fork prong pierced into the edge of her foot, the pain seared down to her toes, making her lightheaded. She leant her head forward onto the cold brick to alleviate some of the dizziness it caused.

Below the chimney, the shouting took over the crashing and smashing, the soldiers in disagreement on what to do next, some stating they had failed in their search, and they wanted someone to pay for their wasted time and energy, whilst the rest of the pack wanted to leave, there was nothing else to be done.

Kicking and throwing the family's precious items as a final threat, the group began to leave, yelling several threats promising they would be back and would find the Ukrainian guest.

The family and Maria remained frozen in their statues, too terrified to stir. The sound of boots crunching away, disappeared with a huge relief.

Sometime past, before Kirt dared to creep to the doorway, checking across the yard, there was no one in sight. The air was still, the frightening nightmare had passed.

Back inside the house, Mr Pignitter and Kirt rushed to lock all the doors and windows, pulling closed the curtain hangings on the windows, before they risked helping a terrified, soot covered Maria back into the room.

The atmosphere became a vision of slow motion. Mrs Pignitter was unable to control her tears of relief and disbelief. She guided Caecilia towards her father's arms to hide the little one from her grandmother's upset. Their home had been utterly torn apart. They were completely in shock, unable to begin putting the pieces back together.

Mr Pignitter turned the sofa back over, placing the hole splatted cushions to the seats. Motioning for his sobbing wife and a shaken, hobbling Maria to take a seat whilst he went into the dining room to pour them all a brandy, to calm their nerves. Passing the kitchen, he stopped to pour a glass of handmade lemonade for his granddaughter.

After a sleepless night on the farm, the sun began to rise and the Pignitters continued tidying their home, cleaning up the ruins the Germans had left behind.

Life had to change, the safety of each of them had to be foremost.

Mrs Pignitter had recently heard talk in the village of a scheme called Westward Ho. She'd been told that Britain was suffering from a postwar shortage of labour and would be providing work and lodgings to suitable candidates, suitable displaced persons.

Maria had heard about fellow Ukrainians heading for employment to America and Canada, but this seemed just too far away. She reasoned if she went to Britain, it was closer to home, maybe easier for her to return someday soon, to return to Vasyl, return to the peaceful village, where they had buried their Mama.

With the help of Mr & Mrs Pignitter, she filled in the relevant request forms and Maria swiftly put in a formal application to leave. She believed Britain would provide her with safety and a home. The farm owners were keen to help Maria in any way they could. To help her set up a new safe and secure life.

Maria feared returning to Ukraine, unaware of what still lay there. She was unsure if any of her family had survived the war, not knowing what still existed in the village and if she still had a home there to return to?

***

Within a few months, Maria received a telegram at the farmhouse. It simply stated she had forty-eight hours to be ready to leave.

She had thankfully been accepted into the Westward Ho scheme, and she was certainly ready. She had been ready for some time, hiding out most days, terrified that the soldiers would be returning to look for her at any moment.

As dawn broke on that warm September morning, everyone gathered around in the front yard to say their goodbyes to Maria. She was now a part of their family, having lived with them for three years and although they wanted the very best for her, it wasn't easy to see her leave.

At nineteen, Maria was now a young woman.

"Take good care of yourself, Mitzy," Mrs Pignitter requested. "It has been such a pleasure having you stay with us."

She placed a gold band into Marias hand,

"Take it, keep it close to you, wear this ring to keep yourself safe, Mitzy, so the men think you're a married woman. If you feel uncomfortable, put the ring on,"

At any other time, Maria would have refused the idea of such a lavish gift, but this wasn't the time to be proud. She needed all the help she could get to stay safe. Maria took the ring, immediately placing it on her finger. The feeling was mutual, Maria thought, it had been a real pleasure to be part of their family.

They hugged tightly. Maria thanked them all, one by one for taking good care of her.

Lifting Caecilla and hugging her tightly, she would miss the sweet giggles of this beautiful little girl. She would miss them all dearly.

"We must go," Mr Pignitter announced, feeling sadness in this farewell. "You don't want to be late."

The truck engine began its roaring and Mr Pignitter kindly drove Maria to the town square of Graz, the meeting area that was stated on the telegram.

A journey in silence, in deep thought as Maria looked out over the countryside, taking in its beauty.

Arriving at the Town square, Mr Pignitter pulled the truck into a side street and walked around to the other side of the vehicle. Ever the gentleman, he opened the passenger door, allowing Maria to step down from the seat up high.

Glancing towards the square, they both observed only a few dozen or so other people were there. They had both expected huge crowds wanting to leave. The war was coming to an end and the towns had begun to empty of military in recent weeks.

Leaving Mr Pignitter behind Maria walked over to the square, joining the rest of the group. They were soon instructed to form an orderly line in front of the wooden desks, where one by one their names were ticked off the typed paper list.

The group was then marched over to the train station, placed into a carriage and taken along the rickety tracks towards their new destination.

Arriving at the district of Puntigam, the group disembarked and were instructed to head along to a huge building of what looked like a never-ending wall of a hundred windows. This was to be home for some time. Maria found out days later that they were to be held in this new accommodation until all the other groups heading for the westward Ho scheme had arrived.

The building was fairly new in construction, with what seemed liked hundreds of tiny bedrooms. They were spotlessly clean, clinical and white, with no homely feel to them at all. Each of the rooms contained just two single beds, clean bedding laid in a pile to the end, and a small table stood in between. Down the hallway was a bathroom, shared by the dozen or so residents now sleeping in the adjoining bedrooms.

Maria's roommate was called Yeva, a curvy, dark-haired woman in her thirties. Talk was non-existent between the two. Maria had tried to spark up a conversation many times with the woman, who did little but lay on the bed with her face buried into the soft pillow, often missing her mealtimes. It had seemed to Maria, a pointless use of her kindness. Maria looked forward to mealtimes where dozens of people would gather in the food hall. Large metal trays of tempting food would be placed on the countertop, ladles and crockery placed to the side, for them to help themselves to the food. The offerings were usually some type of meat or vegetable stew. Maria enjoyed these times of the day. She didn't form any close friendships but was thankful she could always find someone to sit by and talk to.

Little did she know this would be a long stay, seeing a variety of seasons come and go, autumn, winter, spring and summer.

***

By the month of July the following year, the facility was bursting, the tiny rooms housed hundreds of displaced persons. Word had spread that they were to be moved on shortly, but they each wondered if that day would ever come.

On 14th July the roll call finally took place for the transport list, out in the street to the front of the holding centre. Maria's documents were stamped as 'suitable for Great Britain.' She was sent off to join the huge group of women that were now gathering at the far end of the courtyard and preparing to leave Puntigam.

In the heat of the morning, she clutched the woollen coat that Mrs Pignitter had so thoughtfully given her. Maria had carefully stitched into the lining, her treasured family bible, the only possession she had from her family life back in Ukraine. The gold ring was firmly placed on her finger.

Her new journey was finally beginning, after more than four long years since Maria left her homeland. The war may have been over, but for her, this was where an uncertain future began.

The large group of displaced persons lined up and together then marched single file across to the nearby train station, to be transferred to a regional collecting centre in Munster, Germany.

Setting off late morning, the journey on the cramped cattle train was difficult. The Mid-summer weather meant the cramped conditions were quite unbearably hot and suffocating, with just one stop off during the early evening, to receive a small ration of stale bread and a small mug of warm water. There was a cloud of warmth held in the evening air and any chance to cool down was missed. The muggy atmosphere was stale and relentless.

Once they were all accounted for and loaded back onto the cattle train, they travelled throughout the night. Maria tried to get a little sleep, disturbed as it was, sitting on the straw covered floor and leaning against the warm metal walls of the train.

The long but cooler night eventually turned to another bright morning as the sun rose again, bringing with it the returning and uncomfortable heat of the July day.

The train stopped several times the second day. Panicking voices and loud shouting could be heard from beyond the metal walls, as more groups had been gathered up to make the journey and herded onto the train.
Disappointedly, the metal doors on the already bursting cattle carriages remained firmly closed. There was to be no

stretching of legs, no fresh air or refreshments and no stops for the lavatory. People had become so desperate they had begun crouching in the corner to do their business and the stench was unbearable in the heat, to say the least.

The train continued its journey into Germany.

By early evening, it came to an abrupt stop. Arriving in Munster Germany, the groups were gathered into rows and columns for the final roll call.

Once it had been established that everyone was present, they were marched towards the transit camp.

Before entering what looked like an old, abandoned factory warehouse, they were instructed to line up in front of several wooden tables. Here their documents were checked over and once they were officially registered, they were sent inside the large, depressing building.

Each of them were thankful to be receiving another ration of rather stale bread bun and an empty metal mug on their way inside.

Inside was filthy, the warmth of the evening swallowing up any air present in the building.

The group hadn't eaten that day, but without any liquid to push the dry bread down, it was difficult to swallow the measly ration.

There was no running water to be found in the factory. Just a hose outside, as they discovered when someone dared question if they could have a drink.

Several hundred people scattered around the building, with daylight beginning to fade through the cracked skylight windows. Most had secured a space on the hard concrete floor to bed down and sleep for the night.

Few attempted to climb over their fellow sleepers. Venturing out to hunt for the water hose, unsure if there would be consequences for their actions. They also didn't want to leave any personal belongings or lose the floor space they had claimed.

***

And so, a tedious routine of sitting around this depressing building and waiting began. Sleep, eat, roll call, eat, sleep, roll call! With the only option of interrupting this routine being to stretch your legs in the gaps between the many restless bodies. Maria was drained. Her hope of a better life had begun to leave her thoughts. She had stopped imagining an end to this depressing existence.

Officers walked around the building, glaring cruelly at them with no information given as to when this might end.

Several horrendous weeks passed, the breakfast ration of a mug of luke warm water and a metal bowl of liquid porridge was being eaten in the main hall of the building. Word had spread around the hall of a busy movement taking place between the officers and guards throughout the morning. Tables had once again been set out in the yard outside. Gossip of what may be happening spread. Could this awful time be coming to an end, finally?

As a few of the officers came into the hall, Maria noticed a new face, a female officer, short in height, but a large, stocky frame and a bellowing voice to match she noticed, as an urgent yelling began echoing around, bouncing off the walls and breaking the mumble of voices.

Today's roll call was to be the final of its type. Immediately after their food, individuals were to gather up any of their belongings and head directly outside into the yard to await further instructions.

With the final roll call complete, the men were instructed to gather at the far end of the yard. The women were lined up in single file, each of them provided with a grey army blanket, an item they would have appreciated when attempting to sleep on the cold stone floor in the last few weeks.

They were marched back towards the train station, where a train stood waiting to take them on their onward journey towards the Hook of Holland, the port where they would soon board the huge overnight ship heading to Britain.

Arriving in Holland, the group made the short walk from the train station towards the port. Maria's feet bounced keenly as she paced along, excitement bubbling up inside her when she spotted the huge sea vessel coming into view.

Ahead instruction were being handed out, too far away for Maria to hear, so she joined the line that had begun to form. She found herself in no time at all, at a window opening to a small, boxed passport office. Handing over her passport to be stamped, she noticed the group heading to the railing that ran onto the ship.

With her passport stamped, she held it tight as she reached to rest of the group, eager to step onto the transport to take her to her new life of safety. The queue behind her had picked up its pace and before long they were all aboard and setting sail across the ocean.

It had been a warm day, but the night air soon cooled over the water and Maria realised why they had been provided with a blanket. Fastening up her cardigan and pulling Mrs Pignitters woollen coat around her, she then wrapped the blanket around her shoulders to shut out the chilly breeze from across the waves. Checking her freshly stamped documents, she realised it was October. So much time had passed in that dreaded building, but she was thankful that she had clothing for the impending season ahead. Maria headed to her cabin, unsure of what the following day would bring. She wanted to at least try and rest a little. She opened the door to her room, a friendly face greeted her.

"I'm Rosa." The girl smiled.

The pair were soon chatting away, giggling as the rough sea caused them to sway back and forth on the huge waves. Braving the cold winds, they ventured up on deck to watch the waves battering the huge ship. As daylight began to break through, they realised they hadn't slept. The excitement of the journey and finding this new friendship had rushed away the hours.

Arriving at new shores, they were warmly greeted in Harwich, by members of the women's royal voluntary service. Maria stepped down the wooden walkway onto the land of Britain. She was met by these pleasant, smiley ladies who stood welcoming them all off the ship, ushering them towards a nearby church hall and offering them cups of hot sweet tea and a warm meal. They had a spark of kindness that Maria hugely appreciated. It had been a long time since she had felt such kindness, it warmed her heart to know such people still existed.

The afternoon soon passed, having eaten the most delicious meat sandwiches, drank several cups of strong, sweet tea and rested comfortably a little. The group were then gathered and taken by train to a holding centre some four hour journey away in Nottinghamshire. to receive further medical checks.

Arriving in the darkness of the night the women were shown to a hall where they were told simply, to get some sleep. Tomorrow, they would need to be fresh and ready for their new lives to begin.

Maria had caught up with Rosa again, and they both lay on the floor to gather their thoughts. Both unable to sleep, they had so many things jumping around in their heads and hoped that they wouldn't be separated for the final part of their journey.

As dawn broke, most of the women were already awake and ready to face whatever became of the day.

The hall was soon bustling with activity as the inspectors called out individual names on their lists to join them for more checks. These checks included, checking their fitness, their health as well as taking a pregnancy test.

Once the checks had been completed the women were placed into smaller groups. Gratefully, each of them was given 30 shillings, with little or no possessions except for the clothes in which they stood, they were also each given a set of clothes and fresh under garments.

The smaller groups were heading in different directions across the county. Maria stood in line to be given instructions on her work placement. She was handed a piece of paper with the employer's name typed on it, as well as the name and address of the residence she would be staying at. It was written in English, Maria discovered as she folded it and placed it carefully into her coat's inside pocket to keep it safe.

Walking over to her join her new smaller group of women she was relieved to see a familiar friendly face, as she noticed Rosa was already ahead of her, beaming from ear to ear when she saw Maria heading her way.

The pair stuck by each other for the rest of the day as they travelled on their train journey to Stockport station.

Both practiced the new word they had learned, a word they needed to be able to say and remember. "Stockport."

9
Fixing Roots

1957

Work, social and family life had certainly kept Maria and Myroslaw's full lives, extremely busy.

With their roots established and firmly set in the town of Stockport their lives together had begun to flourish.

By the November of 1957 their fourth child was born. The couple named the new arrival Ann, meaning 'blessing.'

Sisters. Oksana (left). Ann (centre)
Olha (right)

Paul (left) Ann (centre).
Oksana (right).

Bearing a child for three consecutive years, Maria had three youngsters to take care of throughout the day. By this time, seven-year-old Olha was attending school, herself learning the English language and bringing home new words to share with her parents and younger siblings.

Maria and Myroslaw had continued to use the Ukrainian language in their everyday home and social life, to pass on their Ukrainian National identity and culture to their children, but this didn't help them in their studies once they reached school age.

Maria, more so than Myroslaw had a reluctance to learn or use the English or fully integrate into the British society, for fear that adaption would be seen as a betrayal of the country she had been forced to leave. She saw her exile in Britain as a temporary measure that had been imposed upon them. One that would one day end when it was safe to return.

Maria spent a lot of time at home with the children, whilst Myroslaw had less option but to learn and use the English language as he was out at work each weekday.

Myroslaw was keen for them to integrate, keen for the opportunity to get a good formal education for their children

Whilst Olha was in school, Maria's time was spent taking care of their home and their three younger children, baby Ann, Oksana, aged two and a half and their son Paul just fifteen months.

The Ukrainian community in Stockport had grown, as more marriages took place and each of the families expanded.

The community had come together and begun to hire a hall in Daw Bank, Mersey Square on Friday evenings. This was a social hall used ordinarily by the local bus conductors and bus drivers of Stockport to gather after their shifts. But hiring this hall area had allowed the Ukrainian fathers to meet up and enjoy and drink together, whilst their children were being taught the traditional folk dancing.

At the end of the practise lessons, it was a real treat for Tato to buy Olha a packet of crisps and a drink. Knowing the younger children were at home and missing out on this treat, it felt a special time to spend with Tato. Olha would play games with the other children, whilst the men enjoyed a pint of beer before getting the children back home for their bedtime.

The Ukrainians of Stockport had become aware of other Ukrainian communities forming around the United Kingdom, and they soon began inviting these Ukrainian guests to watch the concerts they had organised. In return, the other town communities would invite Stockport's to their social club to perform their dance and singing.

The women in the community were kept busy sewing blouses and under slips, making national costumes for the children to wear for dancing and would spend many evenings carefully embroidering the material.

The concerts were held at Stockport lads club, Wellington Street.

Each of the community group members had a unique quality they could bring, whether it was organising the events, teaching the dance, playing the instruments, cooking the refreshments. They all had something to offer.

One amongst many of the concerts they held was to remember the famous poet, Taras Shevchenko.

Maria spent weeks prior to the concert teaching Olha one of his poems, sharing it with her again and again until the five-year-old knew the words by memory.

The concert was held in the early evening. The children were dressed smartly in their national costumes. The young girls in stunningly embroidered *vyshyvanka-*blouses, proudly worn after hours of careful sewing by the Mamas. Neatly tucked into layers of material, a full blue skirt was worn over an under skirt, edged with a similar colourful stitching pattern of embroidered beauty, completed by an apron containing more stitches.

The outfit was complemented by several layers of red beaded necklace. Maria added a small layer of lipstick and rouge to Olha's face to add a little colour to her dark features, weaving her now long, thick dark hair into neat plaits down her back. Placing a headdress of beautiful flowers on the top of the youngster's head, she allowed the colourful ribbons to drape down her back to her waist.

Olha was so nervous as she stood up on the stage, but with dozens of eyes fixed on her she could only see one set, icy blue, Mama's eyes. She began reading the poem in her Ukrainian language.

Peaceful land, beloved country,
O my dear Ukraine!
Why, my mother, have they robbed you?
Why do you thus wane?.......

Maria was so proud of her daughter, standing in the presence of so many people, perfectly reciting the poem word for word.

I prayed, I worried, sleeping not, Neither night nor day,
I watched over my small children,
Teaching them the way,
And my flowers throve and grew,
My children true and good………..

Smiling, as Olha finished, she nodded her pride towards her daughter as she stepped down from the stage. Olha beamed. She'd made Mama happy, remembered all her words, but most of all the performance was over and she could now enjoy the rest of the evening with the other children.

As the group grew, they decided to begin raising funds to buy a club of their own. Concerts were a great way of raising money, but this task took some time.

In the meantime, the community soon outgrew the Lads Club. They were grateful to be offered the use of the hall and the playground area at St Joseph's Church, Stockport, for their dance practise and concerts. They had started using the church for Sunday services, as it was now a church within and accepting of their community, so it made sense to use the additional buildings offered.

Once the community had moved in, they set up a Ukrainian school on Saturday afternoons. Here the children were taught to read and write in Ukrainian. as the only lessons they were having in school during the week were in English. They were also taught about geography and the history of Ukraine, their heritage. There were two classes held, one for the younger children and one for the older.

Within a short period, social events became a regular occurrence and there was soon a large sum of money collected from the concerts and events that were being held.

In addition to the monies raised, sixty-five Stockport Ukrainian families donated whatever amount of money they could afford to spare, Maria and Myroslaw, with six mouths to feed had carefully budgeted and managed to save twenty-two pounds, a very generous donation to show their dedication to this exciting community venture. Donations were also sent from Ukrainian clubs in other areas. Amazingly, they were able to buy their own club.

This took a lot of planning and organising.

In 1962, it finally happened. Their very own community club was bought, an old and quite tatty building on Turncroft Lane in Offerton. However, a place quite central for all its members to be able to get to. This was such a huge achievement and showed a great commitment from all the families.

Ukrainian Social Centre, Turncroft Lane, Offerton

Paul (right) outside Ukrainian Social Centre

It was a single-story building with a hall containing a space for a small stage and bar area to be built. There was a minute but adequate kitchen area and an additional room to be used as a classroom. There were two brick toilets outside at the back of the building. One was for the men to use, and one was for the women. If it was cold and dark outside, it would be quite scary to be using these toilets, so the children and women tended to pay a visit in pairs. There was a large nasty dog in the backyard of a house to the back, it would always bark viciously when anyone attempted to use the lavatories, this made toilet visits a hasty rush.

Exciting as it was to finally have a place of their own, the neglected building needed a considerable amount of work doing to make it all a useable space.

As was usual, the community held meetings together to discuss and organise what building work needed doing, what materials and equipment were needed and a rough time scale for completing the tasks, with everyone donating every hour of their spare time.

A committee evolved, electing a head, a treasurer and a club secretary.

Lists were compiled, building materials were sourced and bought, receipts and records were kept and completed, and the work was carefully managed.

The families gathered most nights, the children spending some fun time together, whilst the adults were busy organising the move. It was such an exciting time for everyone. Any spare minute was spent doing or organising for the community. All of them were more than happy to give up their free time to create a community space for them all to share and enjoy.

Forty-six members worked a total of 3150 hours to construct and complete the work and have the social club finished and a place to be proud of.

The building soon sprang to life, many evenings its chairs were full, drinks glasses clinking, excited voices chattering, children playing, music erupting. A warmth of life had been exposed to the once cold and tired building.

The bar area was strictly for the use of the men only. With four tired children to get home and tucked into bed, Maria sent her eldest daughter to get her father and inform him it was getting late and was time to go home.

A cloud of warmth, noise and cigarette smoke engulfed Olha as she pushed open the door to the bar, not daring to step across the threshold.

"Tato," she shouted. "Tato," she raised her voice further to grab any attention over the engrossed conversations. Several Tatos turned towards the doorway, to check if it was their turn to be called, their time to be summonsed home by their child. Downing his pint of beer, Myroslaw had caught Olha in his sight. He wasn't for keeping Maria waiting.

As well as the whole Myron family, most families spent several nights each week at the club.

Concerts, meetings, school, dance practice.

The dancing was now being taught by a Ukrainian gentleman who had been a former ballet dancer. Dance practise took place weekly, hours spent perfecting the moves they were to perform at the concerts.

The school room to the side of the hall was used for the Mamas to get their young children dressed into the national costume ready to enter the stage. Each Mama, a proud lady, encouraging their offspring to do their best.

At these concerts, refreshments were now being served, the kitchen area, although a tiny room, had at least made this possible and the women were only too happy to oblige with the preparations. Maria took pleasure in using her cooking skills, enjoyed the laughs and chatter with the other ladies.

The club held many social events, special birthdays, weddings and meetings and if Tato was absent from home any evening, he would usually be found at the club.

10
1966

The Myron children had settled well into school life. Fifteen-year-old Olha, steadily approaching a new chapter in life, 'a working life'. Each of them made several good friends, both inside and outside of the Ukrainian community. Maria and Myroslaw were delighted they were all making good progress in their studies, proud of their achievements.

Life had become a little less hectic in recent years. Maria was grateful to have been able to start back at work, she had also found employment at Cadburys, where Myroslaw was now working. She worked in the busy kitchen preparing meals for the staff members. She had a real passion for cooking and was often complimented on the tasty meals she produced. She enjoyed the company of her colleagues and was happy to be contributing financially to the household.

Maria relied on Olha to help with the other children after school, until she returned home from her day at work. A pattern that worked reasonably well on both sides.

The extra income made a big difference. They had begun saving again for a larger home of their own.

However, once again, things can change when least expected and the year 1966 was to alter the pace of family life.

As the new year arrived, so did a new baby. In January, Maria gave birth to their fifth child, a fourth daughter for the couple. They named her Christina, meaning 'A follower of Christ.'

As a new routine was established within the family, the year ahead was set to be a very busy twelve months. The family moved house, moving into Richmond Road, Heaton Mersey in May 1966, rapidly in need of more space for the now family of seven.

Maria faced a lot of changes during the year, both physically and emotionally.

Rosa had married in recent years and with her husband she had recently moved abroad to set up a new life. This was a sad farewell to both friends, whose companionship would continue on paper.

The visits to other Ukrainian clubs continued as huge communities had been formed. Yearly gatherings for dance and music took place, firstly in Leigh, then for several years these events were held at De Montford Hall in Leicester.

That year was to see the opening of the newly established camp 'Tarasivka' in Derby. A camp that was set on thirty-six acres of beautiful countryside became the HQ, an incredible space to hold meetings and summer camps, attended by all regions.

Over the Summer weeks Ukrainian children from all different towns would spend their time as Ukrainian scouts. Olha spent a few days at the camp that year, learning poetry, singing folk songs, marching, taking lessons and learning about their heritage.

The children had grown up with a superficial understanding of what it meant to come from a family of Ukrainian war refugees. The struggles and hardship were shared in their stories and also in the songs they sang. They recited poems and folklore about Ukrainians centuries-long struggle for freedom from tyrannical rulers. They were proud of their heritage, proud of their community and waited for the time when they could grab hold of their independence.

Dressed in traditional dance costumes, Olha (above). Oksana (below)

After a short stay at the camp, Olha travelled by coach with children from other regions to Paris, two children from each community had been chosen to attend. It was the first time Olha had left Britain. Although it was an exciting experience, the trip was to commemorate the 40th anniversary of the death of Symon Petliura, a Ukrainian politician and journalist, who had been assassinated in Paris.

Maria was proud Olha had been chosen to represent the Ukrainian communities, although the siblings missed the big sister, and Maria noticed the absence of the extra pair of helping hands with the children.

It was also during this year that a close friend of the family had informed Maria of him meeting up with a gentleman in the Swansea Ukrainian community club. The family friend was quite taken aback by the gentleman's appearance. He had seen those icy blue eyes before and was sure he must be connected somehow to Maria.

The gentleman was known in the community, as 'George'. However, once they had begun chatting, the friend had established he was indeed Maria's older brother Yaroslaw.

He had arrived in Britain around the same time as Maria. He too was unsure if his family back home had survived and, believing he would never be granted the opportunity to return to Ukraine, he had settled in Swansea. He had made a good life for himself, setting up a home with his Welsh wife, Joyce and their daughter Dora.

Maria was shocked, but nicely surprised by this wonderful news, a member of her family living in the same part of the world. After so many years had passed, this seemed quite unbelievable.

Both Myroslaw and herself had written home for news in recent years, but only Myroslaw had received a response and had thankfully managed to keep some regular communication again with his Mama, Karolina.

Yaroslaw travelled to Stockport to visit his sister Maria, meeting his brother-in-law and nieces and nephew for the first time, during the summer of 1966.

Returning that Christmas, this time bringing along with him, his wife and daughter to meet their relatives and share in the family festivities.

***

The years passed by.

By 1968 Myroslaw and Maria were proud to be holding the wedding reception at Stockport Ukrainian club for their eldest daughter Olha. Marrying her sweetheart

Barry, a young Englishman, 'born and raised' in Stockport.

A huge number of guests crammed into the small club after the wedding ceremony at St Joseph's church. Following an afternoon meal, the evening celebrations began. Some good family friends had agreed to play their traditional Ukrainian folkloric music, a family group. Petro played the mandolin, his brother Mykhailo played the accordion, and their Tato played the drums. Bringing together the two communities for a fun filled evening of food, music and dance, quite an eye-opening celebration for the English guests.

Later that year, Olha and Barry's son Stephen was born. A first grandchild for Maria and Myroslaw, the start of a new generation.

As the families continued to grow, so did the Ukrainian community and they were soon realising they had outgrown their small club. A new and much larger building needed to be found and purchased.

***

In 1971 the move was made to a much larger, three storeys building on Buxton Road Great Moor.

The new club was an amazing old building, with its huge hall. Once the stage area was constructed at the back of the room, it made for a perfect space to hold concerts. The front of the building held a long separate bar area, with wooden tables and stools scattered around the dark patterned carpet. A further smaller room housed a pool table and darts board,. Its walls held paintings of the famous poets and writers, Taras Shevchenko and Lesia Ukrainka, amongst others. The room next door had a good-sized kitchen working area, with a hatch window for serving food through.

In addition, there were many other rooms up the two flights of stairs, to be used for all the various social group activities for the men, women and children.

There was a good-sized cellar area off the bar, to store the crates of alcohol and beverages. With a fantastic long driveway and a large parking area to the back of the property, this building had everything that was needed to house the Stockport community members and welcome its guests.

The social club soon became a warm and welcoming hive of activity.

In the early days, the hall was hired out on most weekends to members of the public to celebrate weddings and special birthdays.

Maria as well as several other Ukrainian women, would quite often be found preparing the food for the parties. They chatted their time away while catering for such events as they had known each other for some time now and had a closeness like family members. The money from the hire of the hall was put into the club's fund accounts.

The club was a hugely popular place, and its members were kept busy with events. It had a real home from home feel about it. Families held all their weddings and special occasions there.

Managing the bar and organising the events was voluntary. Members were happy to oblige in the running of the club in some way.

Many day trips and overnight stays were organised. Full coach loads of family members enjoyed time together in places like Blackpool, Edinburgh and Derby. Staying over in guest houses, watching shows like the Edinburgh tattoo. Maria and Myroslaw, now taking their grandchildren, as well as family members.

The club members took part in many carnival parades through the town, integrating well into the community of Stockport. Decorating lorries in an array of colours, showcasing their beautiful costumes and singing onboard the lorry to the beat of the instruments played.

During this year, a daughter Joanne was born to Olha and Barry. A second grandchild for Maria and Myroslaw to celebrate.

Myroslaws cousins Mikhailo & Anna visit the family in Stockport

Stockport Ukrainian Club Carnival float

11
Passport Refusal

1975

Maria had begun to save a little of her wage. Her older children were grown up and her yearning to return to Austria for a visit hadn't eased. She wanted so much to meet with the Pignitter family again. She had kept in touch in recent years, writing letters in English to update the Pignitters on her family's lives. Sadly, both Mr and Mrs Pignitter had since passed away, although the contact she had with Kirt and Caecilia meant the world to her.

They had invited Maria and her family to visit them at the farm. Maria really wanted to return, to thank them in person for their kindness towards her and personally return to the family, the gold ring that she had found safety in wearing. She had always kept it in a secure place for the day it would be returned.

The family set about applying for their passports, filling in numerous forms.

Long months passed and the waiting continued eagerly. When the post finally arrived, there was nothing but disappointment. Unfortunately, the request for a passport had been refused, the reason that had been given,

'They had no claim to British Nationality'.

Maria was annoyed. All those months spent needlessly waiting had come to nothing. Myroslaw though was concerned, what was the reasoning behind this decision? Determined to fight this, he instructed a local solicitor to act on their behalf, paying him money they could little afford, to put in a formal request to become nationalised.

A little over a year later, longer than anticipated, they both received their nationalised certificates and after waiting again, some eight months later, they finally received their passports.

The family, Myroslaw, Maria and their four youngest children could now take the trip to Westendorf, on what felt like a journey of a lifetime.

Obviously, the family spent the evening at Stockport Ukrainian club prior to travelling. There was nowhere they would rather be. It was a grand send off, enjoying a few nerve settling drinks with their friends and all the community coming together to wish them a safe journey.

Olha, Barry and their children, as well as several close family friends, travelled with them to Edgeley train station. They waved them off on the midnight train, travelling towards the ferry port, taking Maria to a place of memories, taking the family to see the scene of the stories they had heard over the years.

Maria had spent the last few weeks packing and organising for the journey. She hadn't any time to feel anything but excitement. However, now they were on the way her head went into overdrive. Nervous twitches jumped around her stomach as she wondered how she would feel arriving at the farm.

She relaxed, swaying slightly from side to side as the train rushed along. Sitting comfortably on the train seat, she looked around. The family were drifting off to sleep with the late hour. Bending down, she pulled up the hem of her trouser leg, feeling inside, just above her ankle bone she rubbed her fingers over the rough patch of skin. Just a memory she reminded herself, no-one could harm her now.

12
Ukraine's Independence – Safe To Return

By 1991 Maria and Myroslaw had become proud Great Grandparents to Joanne's son, another generation of the family they had created. With nine grandchildren, their family was ever increasing in size.

Each of their children were grown up and had settled down, creating homes and families of their own, but the yearning to visit their homeland never left Maria, however Myroslaw was a still unsure of returning.

Maria had been in contact with her family members for some time, writing to her brother Vasyl and her nephew Omelyan who still lived in the village with his mother Anna, along with his wife and children.

After Ukraine's declaration of independence in 1991 and the dissolution of the USSR, it became easier to enter and leave Ukraine.

Maria and Myroslaw were soon being accompanied by their eldest and youngest daughters and their husbands on the plane journey to Ukraine, to spend time with both sides of their families. It was a flight where laughter was mixed with nerves and excitement.

Pulling their luggage through the arrivals hall at Ivano Frankivsk airport, they were greeted by a Cossack, a sheepskin hat on his head, firm brown boots to his feet. He rode around on horseback, welcoming the English and Ukrainian visitors. An encouraging welcome to their visit.

The family were met outside, as arranged by two of the village neighbours. These were the only families to own cars in the village. The neighbours were grateful for the opportunity to earn roubles for providing transport.

Driving along a dirt path lane, entering the quiet village, it seemed that time had stood still, almost frozen the years, waiting patiently for Maria's return. The sun still shone brightly, shimmering down towards the stream, as far as the eye could see. The birds up high in the trees, still singing their sweet tunes. The surrounding meadows were bulging with crops and stunning bright flowers fluttered in celebration of the hard-working hands that had nurtured them. Tired, old Baba's in headscarves shuffled along the lane ahead of them, walking their cows down to the pasture by the water.

The battered old Lada cars pulled over and chugged to a rattling halt outside the house that Anna and Yaroslaw had shared.

From the outside, the house remained mainly the same, although it now housed a small outside wooden lavatory hut in the yard. The house itself had a wooden lean-to extension to the side, housing a basic outdoor kitchen area and stove. With no running water, the family still relied on the stone well, that was thankfully close by.

The family sat around on newly hand carved wooden benches in the front yard, eagerly awaiting the arrival of their special visitors. Two small girls, dressed in their best dresses, matching bows in their blonde hair, danced around with excitement as the car doors opened. Maria's nephew, Omelyan, just a toddler when Maria had left, was now a grandfather himself to the two excited little girls.

The house, although it was still Anna's home, was also home to Omelyan, his wife, their daughter and her husband and children. Four generations lived in one small house, only Omelyans son had moved out of the home, moving away from the village to follow his career.

The warm welcome was incredible, hugs and kisses were followed, with lashings of food and drinks being offered after their long journey.

The family had rearranged the sleeping area for their guests' visit and a neighbour had kindly offered a spare bedroom for the stay.

The village folk in the neighbourhood were all aware of the visit, all as overjoyed as the family were to have the company of these visitors over from England. Many invitations of meals and visits to their homes were issued by the villagers, they were even invited to attend a wedding ceremony, where an amazing time was had.

They joined the marriage ceremony after what had been a three-day wedding celebration. With what seemed to be the whole of the village, the family joined the parade as it snaked through the streets, the march was led by loud but joyful music and streams of colourful ribbons and flowers. The family followed behind the bride and groom towards the church.

***

Omelyan's mother Anna, now an eighty-year-old Baba, was no longer a threat to Maria, although over the days it became very apparent, she still had the same pinching, bitter tongue that Maria had previously been witness to.

Maria took pride in showing Anna how good her life had proven to be and what a decent person she indeed was. Maria noted with a hint of guilt, that there was no room for Anna to sleep, as the old Baba bedded down above the warm stove in the kitchen outhouse, by herself. Maria eased any guilt by remembering the times the young woman Anna had sent her out hungry, to sleep in the freezing cold outhouse, with just the hay to give her any warmth.

As the family were taken for a picnic by the waterfall, before an afternoon tending to the crops, Maria spent some quality time with her brother Vasyl. He had moved away from the village a few years after Maria had left. They had shared a just a few brief letters in recent years, so they had so much to catch up on.

The small boy that she remembered was now in his sixties. Still a kind and gentle soul, he had travelled a distance from Kharkiv to see his big sister once again. He was so pleased to finally be back with her.

They spent hours sat outside together, surrounded by the warmth of the summer days. They had so many years to catch up on, Maria felt there would never be enough time. They shared their memories of the day that they were parted, sharing a silent ache for what they had missed since that day.

"I saw them take you. I watched you leave." Vasyl fought back the tears. Reliving the moments with the emotion he had drowned in all those years ago.

Maria was saddened, catching a lump in her throat. She gulped down the emotion and took a deep breath. It had been difficult enough leaving her little brother, but to hear that he had witnessed her leaving and nothing could be done but to watch was heart breaking.

They shared their stories, filled in the gaps that they had covered over with imaginary thoughts and hopes.

Maria was horrified to discover Vasyl had been conscripted as a Partisan soon after she had been taken that day. He was eleven years old, spending his days as a messenger, living deep in the forest, trying to survive.

The Partisans fought and survived by forming organised groups. It had become evident that the Germans were not Ukrainian liberators, nor were they arriving to help create an independent Ukraine. Rather, they were occupiers and no less cruel than the Soviets, deliberately destroying a culture, religion and forcibly removing people from their villages.

The Partisans were set to establish a free and independent homeland. In comparison to the Nazis, they had few arms and little ammunitions, but they were successful because they knew the lay of the land. They lived in harsh conditions, with no real shelter to protect them from the freezing temperatures and storms in the winter, or the heat in the summer months. Medical supplies were scarce, many died from infections, the cold temperatures and hunger.

He had survived. They had both survived and they were thankful to share talk of their families, their children, the happy life they had made for themselves.

Their happy ever after!

As the afternoon light began to fade, the brother and sister strolled over to the meadow at the back of the house. Maria bent down to gather a large bunch of the wildflowers that scattered on the ground. An array of differently shaped flower heads and the most attractive colours filled her hands. Looking over the meadow they could see the families working together, Maria's family members helping Omelyan and his son-in-law gather the crops. Maria smiled to herself as she realised the two families had finally come together and once again become one.

Vasyl s time as a Partisan messenger

Maria returning to her home in Ukraine

Maria linked an arm through Vasyl's as they strolled steadily together along the lane.

Standing closely, their heads bowed as they read the inscription, they felt it.

They were silent, but they both knew. They were home.

"God bless you Mama," Maria whispered, bending to place the flowers beside the headstone of the grave.

"God Bless us all."

About the Author

Joanne was born & raised in Stockport. A third generation Ukrainian, the granddaughter of Ukrainian grandparents.

Raised in a culture rich family, she has always taken a passionate interest in her heritage and has studied her family history for many years.

Her grandparents came to England after the end of WW2.

Her grandmother 'Baba' as a displaced person after being taken from her home in Ukraine by the Germans for forced labour.

Her grandfather 'Didi' was a survivor of Auschwitz and was a prisoner of war at the end of WW2.

Joanne has always been fiercely proud of her Ukrainian heritage. In recent years, since the onset of the Russian invasion on Ukraine, she has been largely involved in collecting, delivering and distributing aid to the people of Ukraine and raising funds for a bomb struck orphanage.

Witnessing refugees fleeing their country in a frantic state, inspired Joanne to write her grandparent's story.

'Far from the meadows of Ukraine.'

Printed in Great Britain
by Amazon